Heidegger

T0339089

INSURRECTIONS:
Critical Studies in Religion, Politics, and Culture

INSURRECTIONS:

CRITICAL STUDIES IN RELIGION, POLITICS, AND CULTURE
Slavoj Žižek, Clayton Crockett, Creston Davis, Jeffrey W. Robbins, Editors

The intersection of religion, politics, and culture is one of the most discussed areas in theory today. It also has the deepest and most wide-ranging impact on the world. Insurrections: Critical Studies in Religion, Politics, and Culture will bring the tools of philosophy and critical theory to the political implications of the religious turn. The series will address a range of religious traditions and political viewpoints in the United States, Europe, and other parts of the world. Without advocating any specific religious or theological stance, the series aims nonetheless to be faithful to the radical emancipatory potential of religion.

For the list of titles in this series, see page 93

Heidegger
His Life & His Philosophy

ALAIN BADIOU *&* BARBARA CASSIN

TRANSLATED BY *Susan Spitzer*
INTRODUCTION BY *Kenneth Reinhard*

COLUMBIA UNIVERSITY PRESS NEW YORK

Columbia University Press
Publishers Since 1893
New York   Chichester, West Sussex
cup.columbia.edu

Heidegger: Le Nazisme, les femmes, et les philosophes
copyright © 2010 Librarie Arthème Fayard
English translation and introduction
copyright © 2016 Columbia University Press

Library of Congress Cataloging-in-Publication Data
Names: Badiou, Alain, author. | Cassin, Barbara, author.
Title: Heidegger : his life and philosophy / Alain Badiou and Barbara Cassin ; translated by Susan
    Spitzer ; introduction by Kenneth Reinhard.
Other titles: Heidegger. English
Description: New York : Columbia University Press, 2016. | Series: Insurrections: critical studies in
    religion, politics, and culture | Includes bibliographical references and index.
Identifiers: LCCN 2016002657| ISBN 9780231157964 (cloth) | ISBN 9780231157971 (pbk.) | ISBN
    9780231542241 (e-book)
Subjects: LCSH: Heidegger, Martin, 1889–1976—Relations with women. | Heidegger, Martin,
    1889–1976—Political and social views. | National socialism and philosophy.
Classification: LCC B3279.H49 B24413 2016 | DDC 193 [B] —dc23
LC record available at https://lccn.loc.gov/2016002657

Cover & interior design by Martin N. Hinze.

Contents

Introduction   VII

KENNETH REINHARD

1. The Heidegger "Affair"   I

    LOCAL DISAGREEMENT 1

    LOCAL DISAGREEMENT 2

    LOCAL DISAGREEMENT 3

2. About the Uses of the Word *Jew*   17

    LOCAL DISAGREEMENT 4

3. About Nazism   29

4. Planetary Prose in the German Provinces   35

5. Heidegger's Women   39

    HYPOTHESES 1, BARBARA CASSIN

    HYPOTHESES 2, ALAIN BADIOU

6. Maneuvering and Career   49

7. Couples from France and Germany   53

8. Linguistic Transfiguration   59

Notes   63

Bibliography   77

Index   81

Introduction

KENNETH REINHARD

Alain Badiou and Barbara Cassin's *Heidegger: His Life and His Philosophy* began life as the introduction to the 2007 French edition of Martin Heidegger's letters to his wife, Elfride, originally published in 2005 in German as *Mein liebes Seelchen! Briefe Martin Heideggers an seine Frau Elfride 1915–1970*, and translated into French as *Ma chère petite âme: Lettres de Martin Heidegger à sa femme Elfride 1915–1970*. An English edition appeared in 2010 as *Letters to His Wife: 1915–1970* (dropping the original's "My Dear Little Soul," Heidegger's term of endearment for Elfride). After the Heidegger estate objected to Badiou and Cassin's introduction and initiated legal action, the French publishers, Seuil, withdrew the volume. Badiou and Cassin decided to expand their introduction and publish it separately, and the result is this little book.

In its present form, separate from the volume of correspondence that it originally introduced, the book serves as Badiou and Cassin's response to some key issues concerning Heidegger that emerge in and around the letters: Heidegger's Nazism, his anti-Semitism, his relationships with women, and the relationship (or lack thereof) between philosophy and politics more generally. For the most part, the book is written in a single voice, but it is punctuated by "local disagreements," where differences emerge between the two philosophers concerning Heidegger. Despite these disagreements, Badiou and Cassin agree about two basic questions: Heidegger was probably the most important philosopher of the twentieth century and he was a Nazi, although not an especially significant one. The issues on which they concur may not seem controversial, but in fact they define a careful middle path between the extreme positions held by a number of recent critics, especially in France, some who have denounced Heidegger's philosophy as worthless, because saturated with his National Socialism, and others who minimize his involvement with the Nazi Party and refuse any connection between it and his philosophy. We might call such extreme positions synecdochal insofar as they isolate one aspect of Heidegger's thought and take it to instantiate the whole, whether for better or worse. As Cassin puts it, Heidegger's thinking, like that of all major philosophers, should be assumed to be "fractal": every part is singular, infinitely nuanced, and solicits our always closer attention. We should neither reject Heidegger's philosophy merely on account of his political activities nor refuse to take his politics into account when examining his philosophy

Neither Badiou nor Cassin can be called a Heideggerian, by any stretch of the imagination, but each has had a significant relationship with Heidegger's work and, in Cassin's case, with Heidegger himself. In 1969, when Cassin was in her early twenties, she was invited by François Fédier to participate in Heidegger's small private seminar, hosted by the poet René Char in the town of Le Thor in the south of France. Describing her experience in the seminar in an interview with Nicolas Truong, Cassin remarks, "As Hannah Arendt said, before I was treated as a Jew, I didn't know that I was one."[1] Cassin's position in the seminar was no doubt complex: whereas her fellow seminarians may have assigned Cassin the rather familiar Arendtian role of the beautiful and brilliant Jewish philosopher, a local villager who saw her at breakfast with Heidegger spat at her for consorting with a notorious Nazi. For Cassin, the seminar's dominant tension was a function of Char and Heidegger themselves: the effusive French poet and member of the Resistance, on the one hand, and the reserved German philosopher and member of the Nazi party, on the other. It was, we might say, the dialectic between them that provided the initial vector of Cassin's later path through the history of philosophy by way of the poetic and rhetorical swerve of the Sophists, a path she calls, as distinct from ontology, *logology*.

Cassin describes the fundamental assumption of ontological philosophy in terms of what she calls the "decision on meaning," in the expression that serves as a title for her translation of and commentary on Book Gamma (4) of Aristotle's *Meta-physics*.[2] Aristotle establishes ontological reason or metaphysics there on the basis of the principle of noncontradiction, which in this context is the assertion that "the same attribute cannot at the same time belong and not belong to the same subject in the same respect," which he calls "the most certain of all principles."[3] This principle cannot be demonstrated, Aristotle writes, but must be assumed. Those who believe there is some other more basic principle, however, can be refuted by negative demonstration, but only if they are willing to argue, that is, to *speak*; for the person who refuses to engage in reasonable discourse is, in a line that Cassin returns to frequently, "no better than a mere plant." Thus the possibility of either accepting or rejecting this foundational metaphysical assertion depends on a theory of human communication; as Aristotle continues, "The starting-point for all such arguments . . . [is] that he shall say something which is significant both for himself and for another." The principle of noncontradiction requires the assumption of linguistic stability, that a word means the same thing for two different people or for one person at two different times. Aristotle excludes speaking for other reasons—e.g., to persuade, to equivocate, or just for the pleasure of speaking—as mere sophistry; indeed to speak in such a way is to be not fully human, no better than a "plant." What Cassin calls logology (a term she borrows from Novalis) begins with the assumption that language is not primarily an act of communication, but a *performance*: rather than describing something, language first of all does or makes something in a world. If Heidegger led Cassin to investigate the pre-Socratics, Char's influence gave her some poetic distance from the ontology that Heidegger developed from them. It is the "subversive supplementation" of Heidegger with the Sophists—and their rhetorical excess of meaning—that allows Cassin to align herself with Heidegger's deconstruction of metaphysics without, for that, becoming a Heideggerian.

Whereas Heidegger serves as a point of departure for Cassin's theory of logology (both a beginning and a mark of her difference from that beginning), for Badiou Heidegger is more like a fellow explorer through the realm of ontology, one, however, who blazes an entirely different trail.[4] There are some clear points of agreement between them—for example, their hostility toward sophistry, their insistence on the distinction between truth and knowledge, and of course the primacy for each of the question of being—but finally Badiou's understandings of ontology and truth have little in common with Heidegger's. In the very first statement of *Being and Event*, Badiou grants that "Heidegger is the last universally recognizable philosopher" today—but we may wonder if this is merely an acknowledgment of the undeniable status of Heidegger's work or a more pointed comment about the Heideggerian limitations of contemporary philosophy.⁵ Badiou continues, "With Heidegger, I will claim that it is from the angle [*du biais*] of the ontological question that the re-qualification of philosophy as such can be sustained" (translation modified). For Heidegger, ontological difference is the essence of philosophy and must be retrieved from its metaphysical obfuscation. But Badiou's account of the relationship of ontology and philosophy is crucially different: for Badiou, ontology is neither the foundation nor the essence of philosophy, but the *angle* or direction from which philosophy emerges and from which it must be approached in order to be "*re*-qualified" in its own distinctive terms. Badiou's project receives its direction from ontology, but only on the way to philosophy itself. For Badiou, being is multiple ("there is no One"), a multiple of multiples whose substance is the void, hence ontology is entirely the work of mathematics. This leaves philosophy free to pursue its own work, which involves the elaboration in a particular historical situation or world of the compossibility of philosophy's four conditions—science, art, politics, and love—and the four distinct types of truths they produce.

Early in *Being and Event*, Badiou expresses admiration for Heidegger as "the first to subtract [truth] from knowledge" (3), and, as we said, a distinction between knowledge and truth—albeit not the same distinction that Heidegger makes—is key for Badiou as well. Heidegger retrieves from the pre-Socratics a notion of truth as the self-"unconcealing" (*aletheia*) of beings or being as such, an unconcealing that always emerges in relation to its fundamental concealedness. For Heidegger, this pre-Socratic account of the truth of being was forgotten when Plato placed truth under the authority of the Idea and relegated appearing to the status of lack of being. According to Heidegger, Plato's notion of "truth" is not concerned with the nature of beings themselves, but refers to a function of judgment involving the comparison between a representation and a thing by means of a concept. This "metaphysical" account of truth as conceptual mediation will finally become, according to Heidegger, knowledge as technicity in modern epistemology and science. For Badiou, however, truth is neither classical *adequatio* (which he insists is not to be associated with Plato) nor the Heideggerian account of the unconcealedness of being, but an activity or process of elaboration of the consequences of the interruption or decompletion of being by what he calls an *event*. And whereas for Heidegger mathematics is part of the metaphysical history of the forgetting of being, a scientistic mode of knowledge as "calculation," with no access to truth, for Badiou mathematics models both the ontological unfolding of being and the opportunities for transformation that emerge from being's evental suspension. Badiou's project involves unbinding "the Heideggerian connection between being and truth" and instead demonstrating the connection between truth and the *subject*, which, he writes, is a "*fragment of the process of a truth*," a local instantiation of a larger collective truth procedure (15). For Heidegger, human being or *Dasein* is distinctive in being localized "there," in a world, as the site of the question of being; the subject, on the other hand, is a fundamentally metaphysical category, hypostasized by its relationship to objects in the world. Badiou's subject is like *Dasein* insofar as it also implies a "localization," but whereas, for Heidegger, *Dasein* is the localization of *being* (the being-*there*) in a world, for Badiou, the subject is the localization of a truth. If, for Badiou, truth constitutes a hole in knowledge, an indiscernible and generic set of elements that is inexistent as far as conventional knowledge is concerned, we might say that the subject is the localization of that hole. Unlike *Dasein*, the Badiouian subject is not merely "in" a world, but enacts the *torsion* through which one world transforms into another.[6]

Badiou's most sustained account of his difference with Heidegger in *Being and Event* comes in Meditation 11, "Nature: Poem or Matheme?," where he discusses Heidegger's claim that the metaphysical forgetting of being begins with Plato's repudiation of poetry in favor of mathematical and dialectical reason. Badiou agrees with Heidegger that the poem is an absolutely originary thought, the letting be of appearing; but he insists that it is certainly not unique to Greece (occurring also in China, India, and elsewhere) and that it does not constitute the essence of the Greek philosophical event. As Badiou writes, "The Greeks did not invent the poem. Rather, they *interrupted* the poem with the matheme."[7] And this is the crucial difference: for Heidegger, being is originally unconcealed by poetry and then forgotten by the metaphysical tradition established by Plato on the model of mathematical reason; for Badiou, ontology is determined as mathematics in the same gesture whereby Plato relegates poetry to the status of a (problematic) condition of, and rival to, philosophy. In the very last passages of *Being and Event*, Badiou suggests that this reassignment of the work of ontology to mathematics leads to a completely new account of the history of philosophy, one undetermined by the horizon of metaphysics or its deconstruction: "It is possible to reinterrogate the entire history of philosophy, from its Greek origins on, according to the hypothesis of a mathematical regulation of the ontological question. One would then see a continuity and a periodicity unfold quite different to that deployed by Heidegger" (435). This new history of philosophy would retrieve fragments of the truths that emerge in the decompletion of being in the wake of events, and elaborate the infinite possibilities of their localization in new subjectivities.[8] Such a history would emerge from the "angles," so to speak, of Euclid, Archimedes, Brahmagupta, Fermat, Euler, Riemann, Cantor, Gödel, Cohen, and many others, but it would not be a history of mathematics.

The primary point of "controversy" between Cassin and
Badiou concerns Heidegger's relationship with politics and,
more generally, the relationship between politics and philosophy. In their joint text, Cassin and Badiou describe Heidegger's
"fascination with [political] action and power" as "circumstantial"—but Cassin immediately demurs, wondering whether in
fact Heidegger's investment in political power and its disjunc-
tion from his philosophical thinking was actually "essential."
Cassin refers to a position she attributes to Hannah Arendt
(who will remain a central point of reference throughout for
both Cassin and Badiou) that, as a rule, great thinkers are
not politically respectable: in Aristotle's distinction, they may
possess *sophia*, wisdom, but lack *phronesis*, political savvy or
prudence. And Badiou, for his part, agrees with Cassin that
"political philosophy" is a "meaningless category," although for
quite different reasons: for Badiou, it is not that politics and
philosophy involve incommensurable modes of knowledge
(*phronesis* and *sophia*), but that only politics is a "truth procedure," the investigation and elaboration of the consequences
of an eventual rupture of being. Philosophy assists politics, by
describing and evaluating the truths it produces, but it produces
no truths of its own, whether as *sophia* or *phronesis*. Politics
has no need of philosophy, since it is completely absorbed in
the protocols of decision, organization, and activism through
which it constitutes political truths. So for Badiou there is no

essential connection between Heidegger's philosophy and his political activities, it is indeed only "circumstantial." And Cassin, for her part, insists that Badiou's account of politics as a truth procedure is precisely the problem in Plato and Heidegger as well; she agrees that Heidegger's philosophy does not "derive" from his politics, but warns of the danger that arises when the philosopher engages in political speculation and brings with him the self-righteous conviction of truth. Nevertheless, for Cassin what she calls "the informing of the political by philosophy" remains problematic and must be distinguished from political *phronesis.*

Another distinction between Badiou and Cassin's approaches to Heidegger involves sexual difference and discourse. Badiou and Cassin write from their positions as "a man who is a system builder" and "a woman who is inspired by the most subtle forms of linguistic pragmatism"—but these characterizations, even if presented in a collective voice, sound, to my ear, more like Badiou than Cassin: the "we" remains a heterogeneous mixture of two subjects. Moreover sexual difference is, of course, not symmetrical; Cassin suggests that, writing as a woman, she cannot easily assume a "master's discourse" that would speak as if from outside their respective positions. And Badiou grants that they may indeed speak (or write), to use Lacan's typology of discourses, as "master" on the one hand and "hysteric" on the other: the master speaks with authority, but risks dogmatism;

the hysteric criticizes authority, but risks "the swirl of unfounded opinions." Badiou continues by pointing out that this raises once again the question of truths, which must be supported, against the rising tide of "opinion." So the difference between their positions can be understood equally as the ostensibly ungendered difference between ontology and logology or as the explicitly gendered difference between master and hysteric. Can we say, then, that from the perspective of the man the primary difference must (naturally) appear to be that between ontology and logology, whereas for the woman the primary difference is (obviously) that between man and woman? But perhaps this would already be to grant the sexual-discursive difference priority; wouldn't it make just as much sense from the other perspective, insofar as the ontologist of the multiple would appear to be aligned with feminine multiplicity, and the logologist would seem to require supreme confidence in the authority of the master's signifier?

Badiou and Cassin are well aware of the complex dynamics of sexual difference that informs Heidegger's letters to his wife, which their own discourse cannot evade, and perhaps reflects in the distinction between ontology and logology. But finally these differences can be subsumed as variations on a yet more fundamental difference, which we find in the title of Badiou and Cassin's original introduction to the French translation of the letters, "On the Creative Correlation Between

the Great and the Little."⁹ The asymmetry of the "Great" and
the "Little" appears first of all in the original German title
of the correspondence, in Heidegger's term of endearment
for Elfride, *Seelchen*, "little soul." It appears throughout the
letters in the flux between Heidegger's sense of his "great"
philosophical work and the innumerable "little" (even petty)
academic struggles and quotidian obstacles that threaten to
interfere with it. This is what is most fascinating about the
correspondence, according to Badiou and Cassin: "it extends
this matrix (the Little as the existential basis of the Great) to
many other aspects of the thinker's life," allowing him to sustain
contradictions between the work of philosophy and the facts
of managing a Nazi university, between what he saw as the
singular sanctity of his marriage with Elfride and his myriad
affairs with increasingly younger women. This is, moreover, a
question of critical perspective: how do we judge the relative
magnitudes of Heidegger's Nazism, his anti-Semitism, his sexism
and sexual voracity, his philosophy? Does the "great" simply
outweigh the "little"—render it negligible—or is the "little"
itself the condition of the "great"—whether as the "existential
basis" for conceptual sublimation or as the repressed, even the
repudiated, that returns in distorted, distended forms? Finally
Cassin and Badiou propose approaching these contradictions as
"the relative yet all-important autonomy of separate categories,
which allows for the universal power of a work to exist along-

side the mediocrity of entire swaths of a life, without either of these categories being able to claim it is the truth of the other." This is the most difficult task of acknowledging the contradiction as such, without trying to synthesize a perspective that accommodates or reduces it for the sake of a tenable position, "for" or "against" Heidegger. What's more, the "autonomy" of these categories does not imply their unity; in separating the "great" philosopher from the "little" man, we should not attempt to see each category as itself simple or consistent, for each is riddled by its own series of scissions between the "great" and the "little," blindness and insight, the extravagant and the parsimonious, the creative and the restrictive. Perhaps this is what it means to read as both a man and a woman, an ontologist and a logologist.

Heidegger

1. The Heidegger "Affair"

Heidegger, especially in France, is the subject, or the stakes, of an ongoing debate. Its focus is clearly the presumable relationship between the philosophical works that made the name Heidegger a major reference point for the whole of twentieth-century thought and the ideological and institutional commitments that, at least in the early 1930s, or even until the end of World War II, coupled that name with National Socialist politics and/or the Nazi state, even though the philosopher never had the courage to explain himself, whatever his private conviction may have been, in the years that followed.

This debate would have remained at a basic level, as was long the case, if it had simply established that a philosopher, however great she or he may be, can be utterly wrong in areas whose reality we know full well cannot be reduced to the philosopher's conception of it. It is not hard to come up with a sort of blooper collection of falsifiable convictions and questionable positions in the history of philosophy. When we recall what was said about women by Rousseau, Kant, or Comte; about Africans by Hegel and so many others; about the Germans by Leibniz or Fichte; about solid-state physics by Descartes or Malebranche; about slaves by Aristotle; about epic or lyric poetry by Plato; or about sexuality by Schopenhauer or Aquinas, we can no longer ask any philosopher to have a respectable position on every single subject. This just means that philosophy is a distinctive kind of activity whose unavoidable relationship with a sort of encyclopedic desire also happens to be the privileged site of errancy.

The debate might also have remained bounded, in a way, by metapolitical considerations, at the heart of which is the uneasy relationship between political action and the philosophical category of truth, or the Absolute. Constructing its concept of truth as antithetical to opinions, philosophy, in its main current, does not readily accept that politics seeks to operate with the total freedom of those opinions and thus purports to evade the authority of the True, hence the authority of philosophy. This leads to the well-known comment Hannah Arendt made in 1969, at the very same time as she publicly expressed her extreme admiration for Heidegger: "Theoretically, the tendency to the tyrannical can be detected in almost all great thinkers [. . .]."[1] This comment lumps Heidegger and Plato together, which is by no means a mere condemnation, even in Hannah Arendt's eyes: "When they got involved in human

affairs, both Plato and Heidegger resorted to tyrants and füh-
rers," she further wrote, quite rightly condemning that course
of action as "disgraceful" but seeing in it, by the same token,
the confirmation-by-negation of the fact that Heidegger was
indeed part of the chain of "great thinkers." These great thinkers, Hannah Arendt essentially says—with the exception of the
skeptics and Kant, that cleverly disguised skeptic—would be
better off refraining from any involvement "in human affairs,"
where it is not absolute truth that prevails but opinion, related
as always to the diverse nature of being-together. In any case,
it is not his withdrawal into thought and the major body of
work that resulted from it, his "contemplative life," of which
Heidegger can be found guilty, but only of the fact that he
felt he had to cloak in opaque phraseology, in which he com-
promised some of his concepts, his circumstantial fascination
with action and power, when the occasion for that involvement
was clearly criminal.

LOCAL DISAGREEMENT 1

- *Barbara Cassin questions whether "circumstantial" shouldn't
  be replaced by "essential" here, given that no "great thinker"
  is willing to forgo the absurd phrase "political philosophy."
  A distinction needs to be made between the idea that "great
  thinkers don't have respectable positions on every single
  subject, which is only to be expected" and another idea,*

undoubtedly Hannah Arendt's, which could be expressed as "no great thinker can be politically respectable," precisely because the categories of "the contemplative life" are radically inadequate when it comes to political action. The exception for her would be Aristotle at least as much as Kant. But does that exception prove the rule? Or does it prove that there are great thinkers who are also great political thinkers because they possess judgment and taste? The division here is the same as that established by Aristotle in Thales' case: he was sophos *but not* phronimos, *wise and sage but not prudent, when he cornered the market on olive presses and instituted the first monopoly capitalism. Except that the fortune Thales then made only took on meaning in response to the laughter of the Thracian servant girl who made fun of the philosopher when he fell into a well as he was observing the stars to predict the weather. Thales wanted to prove to her (it was an* epideixis, *a performance, as much as a demonstration) that meteorology, a part of* sophia, *can enable you to make a bundle, provided you want to, something that the prudent, and thus truly wise, philosopher couldn't care less about. For both Arendt and Aristotle, any man worthy of the name must be* phronimos. *And when the thinker gets involved in human affairs, his* sophia, *as such and alone, lacks prudence and practical wisdom.*

• *Alain Badiou agrees with Barbara Cassin that the phrase* political philosophy *is absurd, but for opposite reasons. Politics, provided it's not reducible to the mere management of affairs, is a truth procedure in its own right, concerning the capacities for collective and organized action and, as such, has no need for philosophy (any more than nuclear physics, for example, or lyrical abstraction, or pre-Islamic love poetry do). The relationship between philosophy and politics in no way entails a "political philosophy" but rather a transformation—subject to the (always problematic and in any case rare) existence of political sequences—of certain philosophical concepts, in particular those associated with the relationship between "truth" and "multiplicity," in the mediation of the existence of a collective Subject. And this has nothing whatsoever to do with "judgment" or "taste," any more than it does, incidentally, in politics properly speaking, which involves protocols of decision and organization in which the leading role is played not by the spectator, of course, but by the militant. The fact that when philosophers "get involved in human affairs," as Hannah Arendt puts it, they are just like everyone else, is self-evident. Do we require a philosopher who speaks about poetry to be a good poet or even to be a first-rate mathematician if she or he speaks about mathematics? Heidegger's properly political commitment, if measured against his philosophy, was therefore "circumstantial." For Hannah Arendt herself, we should note, this type of commitment is fundamentally different from the "withdrawal" in which philosophical concepts are reflected upon. As regards Heidegger, moreover, the components of his basic philosophy existed long before his Nazi political activism and therefore could not derive in any "essential" way from it. The way in which Kant and Aristotle deal with politics is much closer, unfortunately for them, to a "political philosophy": pragmatic, expedient, indeed irrelevant, and helplessly reduced to mere "judgment" because it is focused on the narcissistic idea that "what's good is the middle class," a class that never has any autonomous political capacity. Utterly different from this is the (quite simply)* philosophical *vision governing the retroactive relationship with politics, of Plato, who is only concerned with perfecting his concept of the Idea; or of Hegel, seeking a dialectic of totality; or of Heidegger, who philosophically reconstructs History, including the history of political sequences, as the historiality of Being.*[2]

- *Barbara Cassin adamantly refuses to absolve Heidegger of his Nazism by way of a potentially ambiguous Arendtian kind of leniency, on account of philosophy understood as being inherently irrelevant to politics. But that philosophy should in one way or another constitute itself as the metalanguage of the political, that ontology (Being, Truth), like ethics (the*

Good), for that matter, should purport to define politics, in short, that politics should have to be considered from the perspective of truth—this is what seems dangerous to her, as it did to Arendt, dangerous, from Plato to Heidegger and Badiou. That is why Alain Badiou is clearly right to stress that, in the generic case of Heidegger, the derivation cannot start from the political and that it was there before any Nazism: Heidegger holds (and this applies to himself mutatis mutandis) *that it is only because the Greeks were an essentially apolitical people, that is, a people linked to Being, that they ultimately could and had to found the* polis. *Yet, for one thing, that's wrong—Homer, tragedy, sophism, and even the Aristotelian definition of man as an animal endowed with* logos, *each in its own way proves as much. And, for another, it's dangerous, and Barbara Cassin has no desire to believe that "where danger is, grows the saving power also."[3] This is why she maintains that, in her eyes, the problem isn't the militant but the militant philosopher.*

In France in particular, the controversy surrounding Heidegger couldn't be contained within the kind of reasonable confines that this type of debate, which is ultimately regulated by an assumed distinction between philosophy and politics, involves. We can't go into all the reasons here for this (as usual dubious) "French exception." One thing, however, is very clear: the whole of French philosophical production between the 1930s and the 1970s, which it would not be an exaggeration to say was world renowned and at times dominant, had a fundamental, even if critical, relationship with Heidegger's project. Suffice it to mention, to confine ourselves to those who are no longer alive, Sartre, Merleau-Ponty, Lautman, Derrida, Foucault, Lacan, and Lacoue-Labarthe (with Deleuze being the exception, something that actually provides food for thought) to understand what this means. To attack Heidegger with the utmost ferocity was also, and even above all, to settle scores with that glorious period of philosophy, a time when there was a strong relationship between intellectual work and revolutionary politics in all its forms. There was a petty, vindictive aspect, combined, as is often the case, with a reactionary impulse, to the delight that some critics took in ferreting out the thinker's worst faults. The fact remains that, here in France, it was the extreme positions of the debate that gradually crystallized into the only relevant ones. On one side were the thinker's devotees, who categorically denied that anything in his life any more than in his philosophy was in any way connected with Nazism. On the other side were those who held that Heidegger was a thoroughgoing ideologue of Nazism or even the overt and covert inspirer of its worst aspects. In their opinion, as a result, he is completely discredited as a philosopher and should be removed from the academic curriculum in every democratic

country. To make clear what was involved, let us just mention
the diehard defense counsel François Fédier and the ruthless
prosecutor Emmanuel Faye.[4]

Once can note here the traditional point in common, which
the laws of the dialectic always require us to discern between
two extreme positions, namely, the characterization of the object
of the controversy as indivisible. For one group of people, it is
necessarily in his totality that the thinker dominated his century, and he therefore cannot have been involved in either the
abjection or the crimes of his times. For the other group, it is
also in his totality that the Nazi thoroughly destroyed his claim
to philosophy. Doesn't Emmanuel Faye think that Heidegger's
project can be *defined* as "the introduction of Nazism into
philosophy?" That's a bit like defining Plato as the introduction
into philosophy of a Sicilian type of fascism—which, by the
way, is pretty much Karl Popper's position.

LOCAL DISAGREEMENT 2

- *Barbara Cassin then raises the question: Sicilian fascism or
  the philosopher-king? Nazism or the history of the meaning
  of being (hence* Gelassenheit, *the pervasive serenity of the
  existential shepherd, and* Selbstbehauptung, *the self-assertion
  of the German university). Which is Arendt's real accusa-
  tion? We shouldn't end up in the position of the* valet de
  chambre.[5] *The truth of the matter is that we should consider*

each philosopher or thinker as uniquely fractal. But if we subsume him or her under the One, then he or she should be regarded in terms of his or her greatest One, and the critics should be granted the possibility that this indeed is the way he or she is.

- *Alain Badiou points out that Hannah Arendt herself speaks about Plato's (and Heidegger's) involvement in "human affairs" and therefore refers to precise circumstances, the nature of which, in her own opinion, is heterogeneous to everything called for by the philosopher's "withdrawal." She maintains that everything Heidegger (or Plato) was able to achieve in the context of such a withdrawal was crucial for the history of thought. In her opinion, Heidegger was the key philosopher of the twentieth century. It would thus be incompatible with Arendt's view to look for traces, or even proofs or reflections, of his empirical commitment to Nazism in all his concepts. Likewise, there is no valid deduction or natural transition between the education of Plato's guardians—the figure of the communism of the Idea or the figure of philosophy as the subjective form befitting a community worthy of the name (i.e., freed from the principle of self-interest)—on the one hand, and the attempt to become the intellectual adviser to the man he hoped might become an enlightened despot in Sicily on the other. It is as if one were to seek in Diderot's concepts a way of (re)thinking his flirtation with*

Catherine the Great and were to end up concluding that he was a philosopher of serfdom. If active politics is intrinsically different from conceptual philosophy, an axiom ostensibly shared by Arendt and Badiou,[6] then judgments along the lines of "great thinkers are not politically respectable" are a matter of "political philosophy" since they purport to describe a political behavior on the basis of the being-philosopher.

This principle of indivisibility is always characteristic of extremism because it merges the One and the Whole: the unity of Heidegger's thought has to be identical to the whole of his writings, thoughts, passing whims, acts, and statements. All you have to do, then, is isolate one point of the Whole to stand for this unity, since it is ubiquitous. Consequently, for one side in the debate, the manifest importance and grandeur of one text or another of Heidegger's makes it impossible for some stupid or horrible things he said or did to be given any consideration, while, for the other side, his having been a candidate for the rectorship under the Nazis and having made some crude anti-Semitic remarks make it impossible for the novelty and force of the fundamental themes of his philosophical oeuvre to be appreciated.

It is true that philosophers, carried away by a legitimate, and even necessary, speculative enthusiasm, often need to be reminded that the One of their thinking is not the same as the Whole of possible truths. All the more reason not to judge their work on the basis of the equation One = Whole, which is responsible for the devastating, hopeless conflict between two forms of extremism: devotion and destruction.

Barbara Cassin and Alain Badiou, for their part, have always thought that this clash of titans was off the mark. The reader should bear in mind that their respective positions in the field of philosophy lend weight to the fact that, on this particular issue, they are in agreement. It is actually difficult to imagine positions that could be further apart, at least apparently, than that of a man who is a system builder envisaging a sort of contemporary Platonism and that of a woman inspired by the most subtle forms of linguistic pragmatism, who has restored to the Greek Sophists all their importance in the origins of our modernity. Add to this the fact that the man is firmly rooted in the tradition of the classics of Communist revolution, while the woman is exploring the new possibilities of a democracy of the multiple. Even as regards Heidegger's status they don't see eye to eye: one of them (Cassin), having attended Heidegger's final seminars, accepts certain themes of the deconstruction of metaphysics and is basically geared toward a subversive supplementation, via the tradition of Gorgias, i.e., Heidegger grafted onto Parmenides; the other, having always remained aloof, convinced as he is that metaphysics can and must go on, nevertheless also regards Heidegger as the greatest philosopher of the twentieth century and shares both his concern for a thinking of being and his hostility toward the Sophists.

In a nutshell, you could say that Badiou is for ontology, or the thinking of being, while Cassin is for what she has termed logology, or the thinking of speech acts and performances.

Well, in these unlikely circumstances, Badiou and Cassin happen to think the same way about the Heidegger "affair."

LOCAL DISAGREEMENT 3

- *Barbara Cassin then reflects: Only you (Alain) can refer to us as "Badiou and Cassin"; I can't, of course, since I write as a woman and am unable, as a rule, to use a master's discourse. Maybe that deserves a note or an introductory comment about our respective parts in this duet for four hands?*

- *Alain Badiou: Let's grant Lacan that in the typology of the discourses the discourse of the hysteric (who demands knowledge and simultaneously rejects its authority in order to push it further) seems to coincide more readily with a female position than does the discourse of the master, who on his own authority establishes a fundamental signifier and seeks to ensure his control over all its consequences. As a result, speculative "masculinity" is vulnerable to dogmatism, while "femininity," which is critical and performative, is vulnerable to the swirl of unfounded opinions. I naturally contend that, under the present circumstances, we have to hold fast to truths, their existence, and their effects, given that the circulation and communication of opinions are turning the most important of our intellectual fetishes, "freedom of opinion," into the epitome of meaninglessness. Saying "Cassin and Badiou contend that" does in fact contrast, owing to a certain high-handedness, with the friendly, congenial, humble "Barbara Cassin and her friend and colleague Alain Badiou would be quite happy to maintain, along with other people, and easily imagining that the opposite could just as well be maintained, the point of view that . . . "*

Their ultimately very simple position is that the following paradox must be accepted: yes, Heidegger was a Nazi, not a very important Nazi, just an ordinary one, a provincial petit-bourgeois Nazi, and yes, Heidegger is unquestionably one of the most important philosophers of the twentieth century.

It was with this view of things that, in 2007, Barbara Cassin and Alain Badiou brought out, in the Éditions du Seuil's series L'Ordre philosophique, of which they were the editors at the time, Heidegger's letters to his wife, or at least the ones that had been published by their granddaughter Gertrud Heidegger, from an initial cut that was probably made by the Heidegger couple.

At the time, they wrote a preface for the book, entitled "On the Creative Correlation Between the Great and the Little,"[7] in which they dealt not only with the paradox of the great philosopher who had gone astray in Nazism but also with one very striking aspect of the correspondence, namely, the great philosopher's relationship with women—with his wife Elfride, naturally, but also with many other women whose lover he had been over the course of his long life. Here was the figure of a tormented yet indestructible couple, a provincial and German response, as it were, to the French and Parisian Sartre-Beauvoir couple.

After a number of legal battles, the preface was suppressed at the request of the executors of Heidegger's estate, and the copies containing it that were still in circulation were pulped.

The preface, unlike the correspondence, belongs to us. We have decided to reissue it in an expanded and revised form because our position—still quite a minority one—on the "Heidegger affair" and, more generally, on the relationship between the finite life of philosophers and the latent infinity of their thought will not tolerate that kind of censorship, regardless of whether it issues from one or the other of the established positions or from the old alliance between family and property.

What follows, then, is the expanded version of our original preface.

2. About the Uses of the Word *Jew*

Given how things developed in France, as we have just explained, many readers might approach reading Heidegger's letters to his wife with just one question in mind, something along the lines of "Let's see if there's any Nazism and anti-Semitism in them," especially since the recipient of the letters, Elfride, the great man's wife, has the (justified) reputation of having always held Hitler in high regard and despised Jews. But such an approach will turn out to be disappointing, for two reasons.

The first, a factual one, is that little in this collection of letters provides any evidence of the question's relevance. Neither as regards the uses of the word *Jew* nor as regards Heidegger's commitment to Nazism will one find in these letters anything to overturn established opinions.

Let's begin with anti-Semitism.

But first an overall word of caution. The published volume contains only about one-seventh of the thousand or so letters and cards written between 1915 and 1970. We suggest taking

Gertrud, Elfride's granddaughter, at her word when she explains
the principles underlying her selection, since there is indeed
a selection: "To forestall possible speculation, I have included
in the book all the letters in my possession from between 1933
and 1938. Moreover, every one of the small total of anti-Semitic
remarks or political comments regarding National-Socialism is
cited."[1] So there is silence about the "escalating persecution of
the Jews" (156) in the letters that were preserved. But there were
clearly very few letters preserved: only nine from between 1933
and 1938, even though Heidegger was often away from home
at the time. "Whether they went astray or were destroyed, and
if they were destroyed, by whom and when, can no longer be
clarified today," says Gertrud (xii). Only it's very likely that
they *were* destroyed, and by mutual agreement of the couple.

Indeed, it is known that part of Heidegger's postwar activity involved mounting a complex defense of his position, or
rather his positions, during the war, a defense that clearly
included a great deal of dissimulation as well as reformula-
tions, which he undoubtedly pondered carefully and came to
terms with, of his fundamental thought. Is this something he
should be faulted for? Let's not forget that this man had to
go through the "denazification" process implemented by the
Allied occupiers in 1945. He was judged and he was found
guilty. Afterward, he slowly recovered and rehabilitated his
reputation with the unwavering support of numerous "French

friends," as he called them, and most certainly with that
of his wife, who, by enduring this bitter experience with
him, presumably consolidated her position in the face of the
onslaught of women she was constantly threatened by owing
to the Thinker's philandering tendencies.

Heidegger thus attempted to rehabilitate his reputation
without having to explicitly repudiate his successive positions—an extraordinary feat that he accomplished with great
cunning and perseverance. Naturally, we might have preferred
less artful dodging and more of a confrontation with the real
history of the crime. But it is also possible to think—as did
Spinoza (this being one of his most brilliant theorems), and
as opposed to the mindlessly moralizing atmosphere that had
taken hold everywhere, what with heads of state effortlessly
granting one "pardon" after another and officially sanctioned
"memoirs" coming out—that "repentance is not a virtue."

LOCAL DISAGREEMENT 4

- *Barbara Cassin then remembers . . . A train memory: on
my way to René Char's funeral,[2] I had an encounter with
Vidal-Naquet,[3] who told me that the only thing he didn't
understand/like was Char's relationship with a Heidegger
who never retracted. I replied that, for me, nondisavowal
was Heidegger's one "great and good" action. Nothing had
changed in his thinking (the* Kehre *wasn't a turning of that*

sort, nor did it have anything to do with this issue, quite the contrary) that would have enabled him to change political positions, and it was this that he was acknowledging by not repenting. His thinking was such that it could potentially be Nazi again the next day. He was no more inconsistent in this than were Plato or Nietzsche and was very consistent in his flat refusal to apologize to Celan.[4]

As one memory triggers another, Cassin now evokes this one: the physiques, voices, and words of Char and Heidegger side by side, like two opposing kinds of greatness (and bombast). Char colossal and booming, Heidegger with his modest, fascinating formality, the tremor in his semantemes even more accentuated in that they were translated. A different relationship between the great and the little in each of them, which could be grasped in the metaphors they used to describe their common sharing of poetry-thought. Two mountain climbers gesturing broadly to each other from opposing mountaintops, said Heidegger. Two prisoners, each in a dungeon cell, separated from each other by an occupied cell, tapping out messages to each other through thick walls, tiny holes, and an intermediary asleep between them, added Char.

No dividing them into Nazi and Resistance fighter, German and French, when you hear them speak. No dividing? No dividing!

Consider this: the translations of Heidegger. What Ger-
man does he speak and what French is he made to speak?
Think how, for Heidegger, the style is the man, but the style
of the translation, in French, is much more impenetrable and
oracular than the German style and lacks the hearty affability
of a possible barrel maker.[5] *Heidegger is far from speaking the*
"great German language," if only because of his desire to invent
a "beyond" of academic language, the academic language of
a Cassirer, for example, who inherited it. But how can the
historically called-for language he speaks be separated from the
possibility of Nazism, unlike Klemperer's dissections[6] *or the*
disjointed, ungainly language of Arendt, a polyglot refugee
("I thought to myself, What is one to do? It wasn't the Ger-
man language that went crazy."),[7] *or the* stretti *of Celan and*
Adorno? It is very difficult to determine what sounds Nazi
in the German, in Heidegger's German, and what comes
from the French translation, which was done by a disciple,
not a German specialist. It is an overtranslation, steeped in
the Heideggerian thesis on language and translation, as if
German itself were Heideggerian. Isn't the French translation
of Heidegger a non-Nazi rehabilitation that is even more
Nazi than Nazi for us (for the Emmanuel Faye slumbering in
each of us), the way German is even more Greek than Greek
for Heidegger? Cover that Nazism, which I cannot bear to
see,[8] *and it bursts into full view. Linked to the privileged*

status of the "last-hand" edition, which deliberately lacked
any scholarly apparatus, the pious translation, the very one
that proposes "L'Université allemande envers et contre tout
elle-même" as a title for Heidegger's rectoral address,[9] *can*
only make a French reader, who cherishes linguistic clarity,
note that Führer [leader] *in fact means* the Führer.

- *Alain Badiou completely disagrees with this view of things.*
  He thinks that there was only retrospectively an organic
  link between the "great German language" and Nazism. It
  is both an objectivistic and a linguistic fiction to consider
  Nazism as an inherent effect of the language developed by
  German Romanticism. Let's not even mention Hegel, whose
  natural destiny was the dialectic of emancipation. It can be
  shown that nothing is more heterogeneous to the political
  conception of National Socialism than Nietzsche's aphorisms
  and poems. Note, too, that Husserl, in Die Krisis, *speaks*
  that great language and is as "historial" as they come, and
  yet there is nothing in either his thinking or his life that has
  the slightest connection with Nazism. As usual, language
  doesn't determine much of anything, and, as Plato essen-
  tially puts it in the Cratylus: *"We philosophers begin with*
  what exists and not with what is said." As the translation
  into French of that language is supposedly to blame, it is
  hardly possible to simply say it is non-Nazi and therefore
  also hyper-Nazi. Basically, the authentic French Heidegge-

*rians[10]—whether Blanchot, Char, Lacoue-Labarthe, Nancy,
or many others—were on the side of universal emancipation, the Resistance, anti-Stalinist Communism, and May
'68. The fact is, the retroaction of a great philosophy on its
conditions, its political condition in particular, essentially
hinges on how that philosophy reconfigured the concept of
truth to bring it into line with what was demanded by its
times. And this assumes that a great philosophy is ultimately
appropriate for what, of those times, and built with the sin-
gularities of those times, nevertheless has a universal value.
But there is no explicit trace of universality in Nazism. This
is why Heidegger's essential destiny was his appropriateness,
not for the political doctrines of particularity, blood, and
race but for those of universality and equality. That he is
scarcely acknowledged in this way is likely the case, but has
no philosophical import whatsoever.*

It is at any rate in the context of this long, painstaking defense,
this rehabilitation—after the ordeal and the official verdict—of
himself and of others' judgment of him, that we must put an
end to our conjectures about the disappearance of many of
the letters from the 1930s. Only inquisitors force silence and
the dead to speak. The fact of the matter is that, in the letters
we do possess, the instances of the word *Jew* are few and far
between and very unexceptional, their frequency remaining

unchanged up until 1933. Garden-variety anti-Semitism (the Jews are Communists, hoarders, schemers), with its flip side of intellectual respect (they are more intelligent than the dyed-in-the-wool academics, more cultured than the Nazis); there's nothing the least bit complicated about it. And all of this was against the backdrop of Heidegger's "hateloving" of Husserl,[11] which is obvious but never explicitly linked to the issue. As far back as 1916 he writes: "The jewification of our culture & our universities is certainly horrifying" (28)—and our thinker concludes, by and large, that the German race needs an inner strength to reach the top. In August 1920, in Messkirch, he wonders whether they should be stocking up on meat since there's talk about how many cattle are being bought up by the Jews: "everything's swamped with Jews and black marketeers" (77). In October, on reading some academic nonsense about Hölderlin, he writes: "sometimes one could really almost become a spiritual anti-Semite" (80). In 1924, as he is relating how his colleague Jakobsthal cunningly managed to obtain a higher salary for his assistant, there is a parenthesis: "(these Jews!)" (99). In 1928, while seriously maneuvering for a university position, he writes the following about Walter Bauer's brilliant seminar paper: "Indeed, the best are—Jews" (115). In September 1932, dark times: between the Nazis who are "narrow-minded in all cultural-spiritual matters" and Communism, which hasn't been "repelled at all," such that "if a man comes who pulls the cause together he'll be a terrible force; the whole Jewish intellectual world is going over to it now" (133), while the *Jüdische Rundschau* is so well-informed and of such high caliber that he sends the issues to Elfride,[12] who nonetheless sticks to her own opinion. In October 1933 he rails against the constant invocation of the Good Lord: "We do have one pure reaction & the Jews are now all turning Christian" (140). In March Jaspers, however good a man he may be, is still "tied down by his [Jewish] wife" (141).

After this, there is nothing else in the letters that have been preserved, only one final, indirect occurrence from 1961 when Heidegger is listening, on Swiss radio, to Jaspers's latest lecture on "the Jew Jesus" (280), the founder of the history of Western civilization.

You don't notice the absence of someone you don't know, as we said before; you can't make an argument on the basis of silence. And yet there *is* an effect of silence, considering what we do know.

We know of Hannah Arendt's existence and the letters Heidegger wrote her from 1925 until the last one of the period in winter 1932–1933 (in which he replied huffily to being accused of "raging anti-Semitism"),[13] but there is no hint of her existence in his letters to his wife, even implicitly, via Elfride's jealousy. Granted, this absence most likely had nothing to do with the fact that Hannah Arendt was Jewish. The issue does not come up at all in the correspondence between them that began in February 1925 ("Dear Miss Arendt") and was consolidated three months later ("since the day it all broke over me—you" [20]). No, what is at stake in the blatant concealing of Hannah Arendt is not anti-Semitism; rather, it is a feature we will return to later: the control over a man's correspondence, when it a matter of making it public, by his legitimate female partner, whatever the source—patent, official, or something more complicated—of that "legitimacy" may be.

What the Nazis did to the Jews was known, yet there is not a hint of it, ever, in his correspondence with his wife. This is a significant silence, but, in this case, one that lasted right to the end. How, moreover, should the reason for this silence be regarded? How should it be judged? For Heidegger-the-thinker, as we know, nothing is Great, in terms of the history of the individual or the world, except for the task of thinking, the *Aufgabe* that alone provides the measure, that provides the only measure: "I don't want anything for myself, but everything for the task" (152).

What's more, assuming that in these letters or elsewhere Heidegger had wanted to break his silence and confront the crime, which, after he was found guilty of being a member of the Nazi Party, was something he had thought he could avoid, what words, what reasons could or should he have come up with to mitigate his current accusers' condemnation of him? Would the overall style of his thought, which included a good deal of oracular rhetoric, have been able, without disintegrating, to incorporate public confession, or—let's not mince words—disavowal, the public exhibition of which so many passionate advocates of Communism in France in the late 1970s saw fit to make, reviving the fashion of morality and religion by beating their own, or other people's, chests? Which, by the way, taught us that, in addition to their "two sources," identified by Bergson, morality and religion have a third one: the political turncoating of "revolutionaries" when they realize that, in the absence of revolution, being a revolutionary brings you nothing but trouble.

The late Philippe Lacoue-Labarthe, someone who could never be suspected of mindless anti-Heideggerianism, but who instead provided a compelling, comprehensive analysis of the Heidegger case in a number of texts of far-reaching philosophical import, ultimately limited his criticism to the fact that the Thinker nowhere felt the need to apologize. The spectacle of Chirac, Gordon Brown, or Obama apologizing to the Jews, homosexuals, and Africans, respectively, might have convinced him that, on the whole, given the crimes committed, it was better to avoid using this sort of paternalistic, pointless, cheap tactic. The historical question is never one of forgiveness or repentance but rather what, having done wrong, one is determined to put right. In any case, it is hard to see how Heidegger could have turned what he bequeathed to us, the loftiness, or even arrogance, of which is its obligatory stylistic medium, into a new-styled confession booth. It is that legacy alone that matters to us.

3. About Nazism

As for Nazism, we learn nothing from the correspondence that we haven't known for quite some time, namely that, although the Nazis were essentially supported right from the early 1930s by the Heidegger couple owing to their antisocialist conservatism and narrow provincial nationalism, they were, nevertheless, regarded by them as ignorant boors, people unworthy of the heights on which the fate of Spirit is decided. Or that there was subsequently great enthusiasm on the Heideggers' part for the "German revolution" (that was the expression Heidegger used in one of the letters) and for the modest academic and social power it afforded the couple. Or, last of all, that one can catch a whiff of a cautious wait-and-see attitude, which we would say was one sign among others of the thinker's lack of courage once he emerged from his Withdrawal.

Rather, the question is how large a role was played at each of these three stages by a real conviction, the echo and perspective of which could presumably be found in the properly philosophical work, and how large a one was played by social determinations, opportunistic calculations, and pervasive conservatism. In short, what is the relationship between the Great and the Little in this regard? Here, too, what the extremists on both sides of the "Heidegger affair" have in common, in our opinion, is an overestimation, with regard to Heidegger's commitments and withdrawals, of the "great" vision, of radical engagement, of an undeniable connection between what was historial for him and the shape taken by his everyday life. The diehard defenders would contend that, in terms of History's determination by the original forgetting of Being and the role Heidegger sought to play in the reversal of that destiny, nothing bears the slightest trace of either anti-Semitism or, more generally, the whole racialist mythology of the Nazis. This is to forget that nothing, either, in this superb panorama explicitly includes the maneuvering for a position in the university, the little marital arrangements, or the passionate—but also, on the philosopher's part, infinitely cautious—love affair with Hannah Arendt, all of which are known facts. Thus, with regard to the texts that reflect a fundamental "to-come," it was perfectly possible for petty, occasionally very despicable, personal proclivities to filter into them, with the self-serving assistance of family and friends who, unlike the destinal sending of Being, were always hovering around nearby. As for the dogged prosecutors, they specialize in a critical interpretation as perverse and flimsy as the one proposed by Pascal to prove that the truth of the Old Testament was entirely contained within the New. As far as they are concerned, the "great" philosophy is the encrypted text of an overwhelming, frenetic adherence to Nazism. According to these indefatigable exegetes—OK, we're exaggerating, but only a little—it is "obvious" that if Heidegger is talking about lighting a fire in a given text it should be understood that it is really about the purifying power of the crematoria. Aside from how ridiculous a method this is, it amounts to forgetting that, after all, a philosophical text, even one by Heidegger, never says anything but what it says, in a vast empirical context that can always be reconstituted but to which it is altogether impossible to reduce the import of what one reads. Truth be told, as against tactics that amount to postulating a dubious isomorphy between the greatness (or the calculated hypocrisy) of the texts and the pettiness (or the total abjection) of certain commitments, we will propose the relative yet all-important autonomy of separate categories, which allows for the universal power of a work to exist alongside the mediocrity of entire swaths of a life, without either of these categories being able to claim it is the truth of the other. Nietzsche may be right in contending that a philosophy is the biography of its author, but only on condition that the word *biography* be given a meaning such that it is correspondingly false for the biography of an author to be his or her philosophy.

In fact, it is impossible to read these letters as a trial document. The most important reason for this is that, at bottom, there may no longer be anything interesting to say about Heidegger's anti-Semitism and Nazism if we only consider the two dominant positions that we outlined at the beginning of this book: on the democratic censors' side, the conviction that, since he was a Nazi, Heidegger is disqualified from being a philosopher and should be removed from libraries, where he might corrupt youth, and on the devout Heideggerians' side, the conviction that, since he is a very great philosopher, it is impossible for Heidegger to have really been a Nazi. To say that this fight (to stick with boxing metaphors) in which the champions' names—Faye vs. Fédier—are important, is not likely to be decided by the reading of the philosopher's letters to his wife is an understatement. It would be more accurate to say that it shows what a sham it is. For the real issue, which is based entirely on the couple's life as revealed to us by these letters, is the following: Heidegger is without a doubt a great philosopher, who was also, and at the same time, a very ordinary Nazi. That's the way it is. Philosophy will just have to deal with it! It won't be able to get around it either by denying the facts or excommunicating him. We are bordering here on what could be called the existential dialectic of greatness of thought and smallness of conviction, of creative capacity with a universal dimension and the narrow particularity of a provincial professor.

4. Planetary Prose in the German Provinces

The fascinating thing about the Martin-Elfride correspondence is that it extends this matrix (the Little as the existential basis of the Great) to many other aspects of the thinker's life. What enabled Heidegger to be at the same time a National Socialist rector and the amazing modern culmination of German idealism is also at work in the relationships he had with place (the deepest provinces and the planetary destinal); with women (the seducer of female students and the sacred spirituality of marriage); with the university (the never-ending academic intrigues and the prophetic disinterestedness of solitary thought); and, finally, with everyday life in all its aspects. The existential material sublimated in Heidegger's "saying" [*dire*] is admittedly pretty low quality. It is, rather, the processes of his introduction into speculative language, a few examples of which we will now give, that are fascinating to consider.

We need to begin from the beginning, namely, Martin's courtship of Elfride during World War I. Elfride herself noted

that the letters from this period are the model for all the count-
less letters he would later send to his successive "loves" ("The
'Thou' of your loving soul had struck me" [256]).[1] But what
was the motive behind this? Probably the thinker's need to
disguise his desire to seduce and his vigorous, metaphorically
peasant sensuality as a spiritual elevation that turned each of the
women into the chosen source of the work and the intellectual
effort it required. Each time, the uniqueness of the encounter
is presented as a new chance finally given to the grueling task
that fate or the gods have allotted the philosopher on earth,
namely, to save what can be saved of thought in the nihilistic
world of technique. This is indeed consistent with the notion
of the Muse, so aptly described by Étienne Gilson.[2] But let's be
careful: Heidegger is no more of a "Platonist" in the doxic sense
of the term here than anywhere else. Love occurs at the level
of bodies; it appears in the guise of a beautiful young student
or a cultured aristocratic woman; it is in no way "Platonic."
Yet it is accompanied by a prose that incorporates it into the
philosopher's task in such a way that that task is, of course,
galvanized and revived by the joy of successful seduction, but
at the same time protected and kept out of harm's way, since
it is what endures in change, what keeps love from being its
own end. This is why it was unwaveringly to Elfride that the
text on Plato that Martin had the constant intention of writing
had to be dedicated.[3]

In Elfride's case, when Martin was twenty-six the emotional-
ism was not yet of the kind whose force and originality we are
familiar with. Religion played a prominent role linguistically
in the flights of spirituality in which desire was cloaked. The
overwhelming importance of religious affiliations is, moreover,
very striking in the history of sexual unions. Martin, who was
never particularly brave, literally shuddered at the prospect of
having to tell his Catholic family that he wanted to become
engaged to a Protestant girl. It was like an old prewar novel
in which families and religions still kept a close watch on
the course of romantic relationships in society. This religious
factor also determined the sublimated horizon within which
the lovers (Were they already lovers, i.e., before marriage? Yes,
most likely; we shall see all the implications of this empirical
question.) talked about their future in the language of religious
salvation, talked about building a spiritual home in the over-
ripe vocabulary of the eternal *Heimat* in which the discipline
of sexual ecstasy could be accommodated.

One of the advantages of such long correspondences (cov-
ering sixty years, in this case) is that they show the gradual
effects of time. We can see clearly how the religious certainty
that characterized their love at its beginning, and would do so
again at its end, deteriorates and slowly wears out. Particularly
after World War II, following the rupture brought about by
the Nazi era, religious denominations (Catholic, Protestant)

were no longer an issue, except in an anecdotal way. God, nevertheless, remained. The history of this marriage is also the history of a purification of the element of belief in which it was enveloped, to the point where Martin suggests that it is up to them, his wife and him, to create the conditions for the return of the God they talk about. Thus the trajectory of the love letters goes from the lovers' mystical celebration of a spiritual beyond of the flesh, pitting true religion against the profane and degrading course of the modern world, to the withdrawn and solitary creation, thrown toward the future like a Hölderlinian-type prophecy, of the God we are lacking.

This is no doubt why the women required for such a mission were no longer exactly devout girls destined for family life but, from Hannah Arendt to Marielene [Putscher], had a touch of the intellectual adventurer, or the jaded princess, about them.

5. Heidegger's Women

There was one who was "the one," his wife, Elfride. And then there were others, so many others. Still, it is surprising to learn that, right to the end, the thinker of Messkirch and of the mountain cabin had so many of them, and seduced them so quickly, as soon as he met them. From eksistence to epectasy.[1] At eighty-one, "in Augsburg where he had a rendezvous" (315), he suffered a stroke, and Elfride would write on the back of his last letter to her: "His collapse there brought everything out into the open—afterward we were never separated again" (314). Is this ridiculous or tragic?

The two of them loved each other, at any rate, in the sense that Elfride was the home, the place where one is born to oneself, or, in other words, to one's work, and where one dies. Work, family, home: *Aufgabe, Leben, Heimat.* Marriage, from engagement to death, was to be pursued as a "genuine, human" task (84), as far removed from the cliché of the happy marriage as it was from the abominable bourgeois marriage; it was a

question of the *Ur-*, the primordial, the originary; it was—a
metonymy, not a metaphor—a "home that was founded through
our marriage," which "remains the point to which everything
is related for both good and ill" (230), with the unrelenting
rhythm of birthdays ("One of the greatest gifts is that perhaps
in the autumn I'll be speaking in *your* homeland from the realm
of *my* homeland" [273]). A home is something one goes away
from and to which one returns, the old trope of *nostos*. Heidegger would be there very rarely. He was away giving courses
and lectures; he was with other people, his brother Fritz, for
example, cleaning up his texts for publication; he was, above
all, away in one place of solitude or another, thinking. The only
letter from Elfride, which she never sent him but wanted to be
kept with Martin's, is dated June 1956 and reflects the danger
commensurate with the seriousness of an affair he was having
(with young Marielene) that really disturbed her: "You look for
'home' in other women—oh Martin—what is happening to
me?" (255). Home, the real danger, namely, the fact that what
serves as the language of love for them, she says, are "empty
words—hollow words" (255), to fend off guilt and contrition
with an indestructible shield every time he was unfaithful.

Was she an ordinary woman, then, in an ordinary marriage,
who gave up everything, abandoning her education, becoming
a homemaker and having children, "a resting place [he wrote
her] when I return tired from the distant land of the great ques-

tions" (14), with "a kind of womanly . . . participation" (83)? "I should like to thank you for your collaboration. After all—along with the phenomenological critique—this involves just what is hardest: renouncing and waiting & believing" (101). And so that's that, with the self-same sexism, the Little and the Great.

But the Little, it would seem, wielded power over the Great. That is suggested by the extremely frequent use of the adjective *little* as soon as it comes to a woman, starting, of course, with the canonical expression used for Elfride, "my dear little soul," "Mein liebes Seelchen!"² in which the diminutive is already part of the German noun. The fact that women were ranked with the Little, at least as far as the force of adjectivized signifiers is concerned, seems, moreover, to be a typical feature of the time. One cannot fail to be struck by the constant use of that same diminutive in Sartre's letters from the years 1926 to 1939, which were selected, of course, by his life partner Simone de Beauvoir.³ To Simone Jollivet he wrote: "My dear little girl"; to Louise Védrine, "My dear little Polack . . . " And even Simone de Beauvoir, usually honored with the rather odd "My darling Beaver," had to put up with things like "My dear little morganatic wife" or "I kiss you again, my little one" or "this dear little person." We'll come back to this Franco-German comparison later. But it is certainly to Heidegger's credit that nothing resembling this sort of flirtatious paternalism can be found in his letters to Hannah Arendt, even, or especially, when he describes her as "the young girl who, in a raincoat, her hat low over her . . . eyes," her gaze (he emphasizes) supremely quiet, "entered my office for the first time . . . "[4] Perhaps owing to the tension in that love affair and the surprising length of time it lasted, it was resistant to being understood in terms of the Little.

But such was not usually the case, and especially not in their marriage.

Except that there was another surprise—a real shocker, even—for anyone interested in this. The very brief afterword to the correspondence, written in 2005 by Hermann Heidegger, the younger son and executor of Heidegger's work, "on the 112th anniversary of the birthday of our mother and grandmother" (317), was tantamount to a coming out: "Born in 1920 as the legitimate son of Martin and Elfride Heidegger, at the age of just 14 I was told by my mother that my natural father was a friend from her youth, my godfather, Dr. Friedel Caesar, who died in 1946" (317). Martin and Elfride were married in 1917, Jörg was born in January 1919 and Hermann in August 1920.

Elfride was no doubt already, as she would always be from then on, neither the same person nor an entirely different one; nor was Heidegger entirely the same. "That Friedel loves you I've known for a long time" (64), he replied to her in September 1919. "Let's leave everything to the greater course of our marriage" (65), "I trust you & your love with the distinctive

certainty that my own love for you has—even if I don't understand everything—& cannot fathom the source from which
your manifold love draws its sustenance" (65). The new baby
was greeted lovingly, with a freedom of tone and a new kind
of transparency enlivening the language in the letters as well.
Here, too, in an extremely difficult situation, Heidegger should
be given credit for the fact that the multipurpose emotional-
ism with which, unlike Sartre, he emphatically dignified her
affair, rather than shamefully disparaging it, did not preclude
a certain sober eloquence. Indeed, there is only one other reference, thirty-seven years later, to that open trust, to request
the same from her: "Trust is strength in the affirmation of
what is concealed . . . Thus was my yes back then when you
told me about Hermann" (252). On this particular occasion,
Heidegger was hoping to install himself in the unconcealment
of his multifaceted emotional life.

But this wasn't the rule. It wasn't really a question of telling
her everything about the women he met, even if secrecy was
undignified, because "the question of truth & lies isn't that
simple" (254). What we who read these letters that weren't
addressed to us chiefly see is the other women's complementary
function vis-à-vis "the one." It would probably not be all that
hard to establish a typology of these women: they were either
students or princesses, exceedingly young ones as he got older.
Sometimes they were both student and princess at once, as was

Margot von Sachsen-Meiningen, who took his courses in 1942 and was his fixed point of happiness during the war, the woman about whom he would say, albeit only later on and in connection with another woman—Sophie Dorothée von Podewils—that she had been able to make him forget about Elfride. The other women, like "the one," were first and foremost able to be related to his task: complementarity, complicity, and revival of the spiritual through the carnal, which was the sign of progress in his thinking. God and the female saint, on the one hand; the gods, the demons, the Devil—in short, Eros, the oldest of the gods—on the other: "The beat of that god's wings moves me every time I take a substantial step in my thinking and venture onto untrodden paths" (1950, 213). With the exception being Arendt, since it was with reference to her that he spoke about Eros that way, although she, too, was a saint.[5] This exception can be heard at the time of their reunion in the 1950s, when, for example, the sixty-one-year-old Heidegger wrote to the woman who was his essential lover: "But I often wish I could run the five-fingered comb through your frizzy hair, especially when your loving picture looks straight into my heart."[6] The sheer spontaneity in evidence here is something to marvel at.

The unbearable moment is obviously when the only thing that can be heard is instrumentality, as in this strange letter from 1958 in which "your w. Bl.[7]—white but not yet wise"

(267) thanks Elfride on behalf of Dory Vietta and Hildegard Feick (yes, each of them has a name) and uses the "neutrality" of these two women who work with and for him to converse with himself.

One has to wonder here what the word *saint,* in contrast to that instrumentality, means in the speech or writing of Martin Heidegger, when he uses it about the woman he has just slept with, be it Elfride or Hannah.

HYPOTHESES, 1: BARBARA CASSIN

Several interpretations. For example:

1. *She gives herself, and the free gift is akin to charity.*
2. *But why on earth would it be free? She closes her eyes like Bernini's Saint Teresa; she is beautiful and innocent in* jouissance *like the Holy Virgin; she is a virgin in her* jouissance. *Woman's* jouissance *is holy. Regardless of whether she comes or not, they are both ways of being a saint.*[8]
3. *You make her your ally, you implore her, in order to use her with impunity, and, to your surprise, you realize that she's even more of a virgin? She accepts for her body to be used and emerges from the experience immaculate?*
4. *She blesses you? You make her your ally and place yourself under her protection in a quasi-magical or superstitious way? You're little and she's great?*

5. She is your tabernacle and through her you are good like God? Great like God.

6. That's called immediate sublimation.

At a time when Heidegger and Elfride were apprehensive about the churches and the union of a Catholic man and a Protestant woman, which went against the societal-family order, the sanctity [sainteté] of the rite proved this fear to be groundless. It had to be sacred in order for it to be acceptable and justifiable outside the order.

But then why did Hannah also have to be a saint? The order at that time was marriage and the Elfridic home. Did she have to be a saint to justify the irruption of another, no less passionate, love: how can you say no to sacred enthusiasm?

But of what societal and libidinal fears, of what narcissistic sadomasochism is the adjective saintly *the name? Of what is* saint *the name? Of a beyond of instrumentality as a possible category of the female body? Or of the impossibility of facing up even just a little to the fact that there's no such thing as a sexual relationship, even with/for a philosopher?*

HYPOTHESES, 2: ALAIN BADIOU

Barbara Cassin's hypotheses all seem legitimate and feasible. One can perhaps say, and this merely sums them up, that saint *is a translation, fitting to the place and period, of the fact that the female body—as it gives itself over in the sex act and assuming that there is a touch of love in all Heidegger's affairs (and Alain Badiou trusts him on this)—can only appear as a miracle, as the incredible real of a glorious body. And it is all the more glorious in that its uncovering is more hidden, more unexpected, in the ordinary sphere of the visible. Now, in the world of religious tradition, the essential attribute of male and female saints is the performance of miracles; it is even on this, as it were, material, basis, requiring investigations and witnesses, that for a very long time men and women were canonized. Any woman can be declared a* saint *insofar as any woman is capable of at least one miracle, her amorous nudity. Psychoanalysis has established that this miracle occurs when the female body constitutes the entire real of the Phallus, the key to the symbolic order. Women's unconcealment "real-izes"—let me venture that term—the symbolic order as a whole. So let's conclude that the use of religious vocabulary is only a proleptic transcription of the well-known statement "Girl is Phallus," which means that you ultimately get the formula: "Female Saint = Phallus," a formula that is not applicable to the male saint.*

6. Maneuvering and Career

What flows through all these love affairs, in Heidegger's own terms, from the sinful constraints of petty everyday life to the grandeur of the thinking work, from the material of love and sexlife to the conceptual and linguistic inventions of which that material is a vitally important resource, goes hand-in-hand with another dialectic: that of the career, of the link that becomes established between the professorial profession and its vicissitudes and the progress of the written work.

The political maneuvering to obtain a teaching position, a promotion, institutional superiority over second-rate colleagues and rivals, an "honor" (such as being the only candidate to be considered for a particular position)—all this sort of thing takes up a truly extraordinary amount of space in the correspondence. And it is especially ironic since, in the final analysis, Heidegger would practically never leave his native province, turning down other opportunities, in Berlin in particular, for purely conventional reasons he would often change into noble ones later on. It is important to remember in this regard that Heidegger had no family fortune and was really dependent on his position in the university to earn a living. He went through some hard times financially and he had many enemies in academia, including during the Hitler era. His long-standing desire to reform the German university also derived from a personal experience rife with obstacles, arbitrary restrictions, and absurd decisions of which he was occasionally the victim. That's one side of the story. The other is his explicit adherence to the stringent rules of social life in the German provinces, his participation in that blend of conformism and spite typical of the petite bourgeoisie of those places where, during the years in question, religion, social rank, family, and institutions reigned supreme. Here, too, Heidegger transmuted this particularly thankless material into a post-Romantic discourse on dwelling, place, path, origins . . . And, to that end, he elevated all the scheming and intrigues, in which he was in fact endlessly involved, to the level of the discipline of self-abnegation and supreme contempt. What can be read in the letters is a three-stage construction: first, an experience that is often at the level of conventional life and its petty turmoil; second, a subjective, often retroactive, stance that places the mediocrity of this life in a devastated global environment and excepts pure thought from it; and, finally, a brilliant production of language that envelops the exception and makes it shine in the sky of philosophy. Elfride, the "dear little soul," was the designated confidante and no doubt the astute adviser where all this was concerned.

7. **Couples from France and Germany**

It is very interesting to compare the social and intellectual figure of the Heidegger couple with that of the Sartre–de Beauvoir couple.

The differences between them are readily apparent, chief among them being that Simone de Beauvoir was a writer in her own right.

In this connection, one can't help but fantasize—and this is a sort of existential and historical eidetic variation—about what Heidegger's fate would have been if he had finally made up his mind to leave Elfride for Hannah in the 1920s. Some might object that it was obviously impossible for him to do so, for the reasons we ourselves have suggested: his conservatism, true conjugal love, career calculations, and so on. Nevertheless, we can still fantasize about it. After all, wouldn't it have been possible for the man who wrote to the young woman in 1925: "Nothing like it has ever happened to me. In the rainstorm on the way home, you were even more beautiful and great.

I would have liked to wander with you for nights on end";[1] who begged "Please, Hannah, give me a few more words. I cannot let you go like this";[2] for the man who, in honor of their reunion twenty-five years later, wrote to the same woman: "When thought with love illuminates, / grace has given it what radiates"[3]—wouldn't it have been possible for such a man to build a life on the true meaning of these declarations? Only in that case would we have had a way to compare the two couples as to the claimed equality of their respective compositions.

But such was not the case, and the two couples are not symmetrical. As a result, however, their similarities, especially if we regard things from Sartre's (and Heidegger's) viewpoint, are even more striking. For in both cases, around an extremely active, diverse, often clandestine love and sex life, the couple—or should we say The Couple?—was structured as something that guaranteed the continuity of a sort of endless conversation, ultimately imposing its law on the multiplicity that was at odds with it. In both cases, philosophical sublimation countered the passage of the multiple with this enduring unity. Heidegger would say amorous sensuality serves as a circumstantial impetus; only the saintliness of the wife is equal to the finished work. And Sartre would say other women are contingent; only Simone is necessary. Finally, in both cases there is an attempt to establish a ternary set, in which the woman who is forever the legitimate one, whether she is the wife or the necessary woman, bestows, by virtue of her own permanent status, a sort of provisional blessing on the interloper. In *She Came to Stay* Simone de Beauvoir portrayed the paradoxical violence inherent in such an arrangement. Heidegger, too, as is clear from many of his letters, wanted to gain his lovers' acceptance of Elfride's permanent status as well as Elfride's sanctioning of her rivals' existence. And in several cases Elfride herself sought to establish a special relationship with one or the other of the philosopher's mistresses, especially with those who caused her the most suffering. Even Hannah Arendt's visit, almost twenty years after her affair with Martin, occurred under the auspices of a reconciliation with Elfride, who was informed of the facts by her husband only a short time before the visit.

Note, too, that the wife's (or the necessary woman's) life did not consist merely of innocence and waiting. It was a far cry from that in the case of Simone de Beauvoir, whose passionate love affairs are well known. But it wasn't true, either, in the case of Elfride, whose younger son, Hermann, as we have seen, was not Martin's child.

Where all these young men and women—Martin, Jean-Paul, Simone, and Elfride—were concerned, it was the interwar period, the Roaring Twenties, a time when old customs were crumbling, when a new conception of the couple and its relationship with the fluctuation of desire was attempting to destroy religious and family constraints. This was the terrain of existentialism, after all, of a new interrelationship between the freedom of personal behaviors, the power of choice, and the inertia of social conditions. Heidegger/Elfride, a couple of the existentialist era? Yes, in a certain sense. Something was expected of the couple, who were not unaffected by social and intellectual change. An ongoing, multifaceted complicity developed between them. There was the need to establish, from within the couple, a new way of regulating the tension between fidelity and infidelity.

The essential difference between Heidegger and Sartre, who shared many features of the period, is basically the fact that one of them was a professor in the German provinces and the other was a Parisian intellectual. This difference between the opacity of the provincial place and the cosmopolitan transparency of a great capital city can be seen constantly, as much in the nuances as in the intellectual sublimation of their love lives. Calling the woman of your life "Beaver" is obviously not the same thing as calling her "dear little soul." As concerns these subjects, it would be more fitting to speak of a provincial, hypocritical, and religiously oriented existentialism and of a much more open (more cynical?) and politically oriented capital-city existentialism.

We have nevertheless also seen how there is a sort of deliberate vulgarity in Sartre's letters, which is not necessarily any better than German reserve. Aside from the fact that Sartre and Simone de Beauvoir's much-discussed "tell all" policy involved a double standard, in no way did it eliminate suspicious psychological tactics. In particular, it is clear that Sartre related the details of one affair or another with the aim of making Simone de Beauvoir think that it involved nothing but superficial contingency. We readers have our own reasons for remaining skeptical about this incessant propaganda, which, when you come right down to it, remains within the bounds of traditional conjugal discretion. What is certain, at any rate, is that it leads to some really distasteful passages. Who can read without feeling a sort of vague nausea, to use the Master's vocabulary, the account he gives "darling Beaver" of the laborious deflowering of Tania, which concludes with "and from time to time I feel myself about to say, with feeling, that I must love her as I do, having lent myself to the sordid task."[4]

And so, in the end, it appears that a problem remains, since these two couples who were so unalike put philosophical dignity to some terrible tests.

In a nutshell, Heidegger's "dear little soul" [*chère petite âme*] is not necessarily of a different nature from the "dear little flame" [*chère petite flamme*] that Sartre wrote to Louise Védrine,[5] when "dear little" means that a man is addressing his wife or mistress in accordance with a complicity whose imbalances are every bit as coded as they are shared. *Âme* and *flamme* have, moreover, been interchangeable for a very long time. That they are both "little," in these instances, doesn't help matters.

8. Linguistic Transfiguration

It must be obvious by now that it is through language that the transition from the Little's experience to the Great's utterance occurs.

"My beginning is Titanic & it ends in concepts" (19), Heidegger wrote to Elfride very early on, in 1916. With Elfride acting as a vase or a receptacle in this domain, too, the letters are the reflection of the theater of thought, with conceptual characters appearing in the order they were created, at a rhythm that matched that of his courses, lectures, and philosophical works. In 1930, for example, his verdict on Berlin, a place of "sheer groundlessness" (*die absolute Bodenlosigkeit dieses Ortes*) and yet "no real abyss for philosophy" (*kein wirklicher Abgrund für die Philosophie*), transmutes everyday life into the language of *Vom Wesen des Grundes* (*The Essence of Reasons*), which was being written in 1929. Hence the real difficulty of translation, since the transmuted novelty is reintegrated into and reproduced in the everyday language, replete with abbreviations and dialect, from which it was extracted—there is even something like a complicity of idiolects between the "My D. S." ("Dear little soul," 220) and the instances of *Gestell* ("framing," 1952, 228), *Ge-Stell* (1956, 257), and *Ereignis* ("essential event," 186). This is heavy artillery—clearly too heavy when every *Ur-* is translated as "originary" and the perfectly simple *Dasein* as "being-there," since it "must" contrast with *Existenz, Ek-sistenz, Sein, Hiersein* ("being here," 231), *Für-uns-Sein* ("being-for-ourselves," 30), *Wesen* ("essence," 185), and *Seyn* ("Beying," 163).[1]

In a sense, it is only ever a question of language. Everything, for Heidegger, is staked on it, as is shown by his experiencing the rectorship as a feeling of "being drained," which made him fear a long barren period and feel the need for a "new language" (1934, 144). He repeats this over and over: "Increasingly clearly I feel the need for simple saying; but this is difficult; for our language only applies to what has been up to now [*das Bischerige*]" (1945, 182). It was a matter of striking the right balance between banality and bombast in the writing; using everything available—Hölderlin, Parmenides and Heraclitus, Humboldt—to create; even "camouflaging" the pervasive presence of language ("But the title [*The Principle of Reason*] . . . is chosen as a *camouflage* so the theme of '*language*' doesn't create an immediate sensation" [1955, 249]). Günter Grass in *Dog Years* and Adorno with *The Jargon of Authenticity* could not have been more on target, as Heidegger's terse mention of a plot against him reveals (1964, 290).[2]

So, when all is said and done, what is to be thought about the philosophical import of these letters?

The problem hardly arises if you are a Nietzschean, which, incidentally, means that you prefer disorder to order in philosophy. For anyone who is convinced, like Nietzsche, that a philosophy is ultimately a life story, the portrait Heidegger drew of himself for his wife in letter after letter, even if it was also, like any portrait, a pose and a lie, can still be clearly interpreted as an unintended illumination of his thought processes. The move from the Little to the Great, like Plato's move from the structures of the soul to those of the City, was easy. It is indeed as a reflection of the German Catholic provinces and a mountain cabin that the originary, the home, the welcome, or the place must be imagined. It is indeed as a reflection of Elfride that the latent saintliness of the other, the rather obtuse connection between the people and the work, the virtue of forgiveness, stubborn endurance, and even the resolute decision never to give up must be imagined. It is indeed the scheming of colleagues, the hassles with publishers and lecturers, and the newspaper attacks on him that present us with a world divorced from Being by the domination of technology and the power of the worthless "they." It is as a female student that the Dionysian appeal of nature appears and in the guise of downhill skiing in the fresh snow that, for one moment, the degradation of what must be allowed to come forth disappears. It is also in the guise of a professor seized by rectoral debauchery that the redeeming function of the Führer appears.[3] And, conversely, we can clearly see in the horny rector, in the mountain walker's boastfulness, in the suspicious lover of every passing skirt, in the schemer of academic committees, in the husband whose infidelities were intertwined with his fidelity, and in the sedentary provincial something that absolutely exceeds their outward appearance and binds them intimately and forcefully to a new kind of thinking; something, deposited by Heidegger in the crates of his papers and the reprints of his books, that affects us not only because of the sublimation of their latent existential material but also because of the wholly new intimation they afford of the fact that, in our seemingly fast-paced but at the same time stagnant and pernicious world, this philosopher, through the very torsion to which he subjected language, was able to express certainty that the means for salvation existed, right where he was, with his pettiness, lack of courage, stubborn will to survive, and ordinary distractions. Yes, right there, were the means, which he'd discovered: a serene way of living more essential than all his vicissitudes, which he was able to change, as Mallarmé did the console table of a small Parisian living room,[4] into the rarest star.

Notes

INTRODUCTION

1. Nicolas Truong, "Barbara Cassin: 'Je cherche ce que parler veut dire,'" *Philosophie Magazine* 14 (November 2007), http://www.philomag.com/les-idees/entretiens/barbara-cassin-je-cherche-ce-que-parler-veut-dire-4573.

2. Barbara Cassin and Michel Narcy, *La Décision du sens: Le livre* Gamma *de la* Métaphysique *d'Aristote, introduction, texte, traduction et commentaire* (Paris: J. Vrin, 1989). Also see Cassin's major work on sophistry, *L'Effet sophistique* (Paris: Gallimard, 1995).

3. Jonathan Barnes, ed., *The Complete Works of Aristotle*, 2 vols. (Princeton: Princeton University Press, 1984), 2:1588.

4. Helpful accounts of the relationship of Badiou's ideas to those of Heidegger can be found in Mark Hewson's entry "Heidegger" in *Alain Badiou: Key Concepts*, ed.

A. J. Bartlett and Justin Clemens (Durham: Acumen, 2010). Also see Graham Harman's essay "Badiou's Relation to Heidegger in *Theory of the Subject*" in *Badiou and Philosophy*, ed. Sean Bowden and Simon Duffy (Edinburgh: Edinburgh University Press, 2012).

5. Alain Badiou, *Being and Event*, trans. Oliver Feltham (New York: Continuum, 2005), 1.

6. See Badiou's distinction in *Theory of the Subject*, trans. Bruno Bosteels (New York: Continuum, 2009) between what he calls *esplace* (or the "space of placement" in a structured world) and *horlieu*, the "out-place" or "place as out-of-place" (15), whose topology compares with Lacan's notion of *extimité*, or an intimate exteriority.

7. Badiou, *Being and Event*, 126.

8. In *Manifesto for Philosophy*, trans. Norman Madarasz (Albany: State University of New York Press, 1999), Badiou elaborates his differences with Heidegger much more forcefully. Badiou describes Heidegger's project as "sutured" to poetry, rather than maintaining the compossibility of all four of its conditions (art, politics, science, and love). Heidegger's "stroke of genius" was to deconstruct the subject-object opposition, but he was only able to achieve this at the cost of "*hand[ing] philosophy over to poetry.*" Interestingly enough, for

Badiou Heidegger's suturing of philosophy to poetry comes from "following René Char," whereas for Cassin Char serves as something of an antidote or counter-weight to Heidegger (73–76). Comments on Heidegger and interesting parallels to Heidegger can be found throughout Badiou's work (in particular, see *Briefings on Existence: A Short Treatise on Transitory Ontology* and *Logics of Worlds*), but more definitive work on this topic awaits the publication of Badiou's 1986–1987 seminar, *L'être 3. Figure du retrait: Heidegger* (Paris: Fayard, forthcoming).

9. See chapter 1, note 5.

1. THE HEIDEGGER "AFFAIR"

1. Hannah Arendt, text of a radio address (made on September 25, 1969) on Heidegger's eightieth birthday, in Hannah Arendt and Martin Heidegger, *Letters, 1925–1975,* ed. Ursula Ludz and trans. Andrew Shields (New York: Harcourt, 2003), 162. —Trans.

2. The word *historial* came into French as a translation for Heidegger's term *geschichtlich*, from the noun *Geschichte,* which for Heidegger means roughly history as that which happens, in opposition to *Historie* as the

study of past events. The term develops nuances over the course of Heidegger's writing and their translations; for an account of these shifts, see *Dictionary of Untranslatables: A Philosophical Lexicon,* ed. Barbara Cassin, translation edited by Emily Apter, Jacques Lezra, and Michael Wood, trans. Steven Rendell et al. (Princeton: Princeton University Press, 2014), 391–94.

3. This phrase is from Hölderlin's poem "Patmos"—"Wo aber Gefahr ist, wächst das Rettende auch"—quoted by Heidegger in "The Question Concerning Technology," in *The Question Concerning Technology and Other Essays,* trans. William Lovitt (New York: Harper and Row, 1982), 28. —Trans.

4. The defense of Heidegger can be found chiefly in François Fédier's *Heidegger: Anatomie d'un scandale* (Paris: Laffont, 1988) and, more recently, in *Heidegger, à plus forte raison* (Paris: Fayard, 2007), a collection of essays edited by Fédier, who also wrote a foreword to the volume. For the opposite view, see, in particular, Emmanuel Faye, *Heidegger: The Introduction of Nazism Into Philosophy* (New Haven: Yale University Press, 2009). —Trans.

5. Cassin is alluding here to Hegel's comment in *The Philosophy of History* that the well-known proverb "No man is a hero to his valet "was true," not because the

hero is not a hero, but because the valet is a valet."
Similarly, she suggests that Heidegger is "fractal, and if
we consider him to be bad through and through, it is
perhaps because we are valets too." He should instead
be regarded as a text, "to which a principle of charity
should be applied, as Arendt no doubt applied one to
him, reading beneath the rector's Nazism the complex-
ity of philosophical notions that, however dubious,
were still worthy of interest" (personal communication). —Trans.

6. Cassin here adds: "and by Cassin as well." So with
this agreement our local disagreement could end, but
not the aspect of it that concerns the Platonic-Hei-
deggerian position of dominance, and, literally, of the
informing of the political by philosophy, as opposed to
a position that she still calls Aristotelian-Arendtian.

7. The French title of the preface is "De la corrélation créa-
trice entre le Grand et *le Petit*" (my emphasis). I have for
the most part rendered "petit(e)" as "little" throughout
this translation, even when, as here, "small" might have
sounded more natural. This was done in the interests of
remaining consistent with the French text and particularly with the phrase that figures in the title of the book
in French: *ma chère petite âme* ("my dear little soul"),
Heidegger's preferred form of address for his wife. As

will become clear later on, the thrust of Badiou's and Cassin's argument depends on this as it were *ur*-"little" that I considered important to preserve in the English translation. See also chapter 5, note 2. —Trans.

2. ABOUT THE USES OF THE WORD *JEW*

1. Martin Heidegger, *Letters to His Wife,* ed. Gertrud Heidegger, trans. R. D. V. Glasgow (Malden, MA: Polity, 2008), xii. Page numbers from this edition will henceforth be given in parentheses. In a footnote, Badiou and Cassin say that the citations they use are from their own edition of the letters: Martin Heidegger, "*Ma chère petite âme*". *Lettres à sa femme Elfride, 1915–1970,* trans. Marie-Ange Maillet (Paris: Seuil, 2007), which included the preface mentioned previously. —Trans.

2. The poet René Char (1907–1988), a member of the French Resistance in World War II, was greatly admired by Heidegger, who gave several seminars in the late 1960s in Le Thor, near Char's home in the south of France. —Trans.

3. A specialist of Ancient Greece, the French historian Pierre Vidal-Naquet (1932–2006) was a politically engaged intellectual who notably wrote about Holo-

caust denial, torture during the Algerian War, and the prospects for peace in the Middle East. —Trans.

4. When the poet Paul Celan (1920–1970), a Jew whose family had perished in the Holocaust, visited Heidegger at his mountain cabin in Todtnauberg in 1966, he signed the guest book there in a way that suggested he was hoping for a "word" from Heidegger, no doubt of explanation or apology for his Nazism, but no such word was forthcoming. —Trans.

5. In *Being and Time* Heidegger uses the example of an ordinary workman, a barrel maker (as his own father was), whose hammer suddenly breaks into pieces, jolting him out of his "everydayness" to experience "authentic" Being. —Trans.

6. See Victor Klemperer, *The Language of the Third Reich* (London: Continuum, 2006). —Trans.

7. Hannah Arendt, "What Remains? The Language Remains," interview with Günter Gaus in *The Portable Hannah Arendt* (London: Penguin, 2003), 13. —Trans.

8. A direct allusion to a famous line in Molière's *Tartuffe* ("Cover that bosom which I cannot bear to see") in which the imposter's hypocrisy is comically glaring. —Trans.

9. This might be translated as "The German University in the Face of All Opposition." Pierre Joris has

condemned this French translation as "a transparent attempt to depoliticize and defuse the title of a text that poses major problems concerning its political intentions" ("Heidegger, France, Politics, the University," http://wings.buffalo.edu/epc/authors/joris/heideggerfascism.html). "The Self-Affirmation of the German University," as the speech is known in English, is a literal translation of the German title. —Trans.

10. Barbara Cassin can't help but insist that *authentic* be underscored here.

11. The word *hainamoration* used in the French is a term of Lacan's invention from his seminar *Encore*, rendered here in Bruce Fink's translation. —Trans.

12. A German Jewish weekly newspaper that appeared from 1902 until 1938. —Trans.

13. Hannah Arendt and Martin Heidegger, *Letters, 1925–1975,* ed. Ursula Ludz and trans. Andrew Shields (New York: Harcourt, 2003), 52.

4. PLANETARY PROSE IN THE GERMAN PROVINCES

1. This is from the birthday letter from 1918, which was entitled "In the Thou to God" by Martin and donated to the German Literature Archive in Marbach by Elf-

ride. On the back of it she wrote: "From a letter from
Martin of 1918, the model for all his love letters to his
many 'loves.'"

2. See Étienne Gilson, *Choir of Muses,* trans. Maisie Ward
(London: Sheed and Ward, 1953). —Trans.

3. "I often think about what I promised you early on:
that the work in which I deal specifically with Plato's
thought is to be yours. If the world stays reasonably
in order and I stay alive & keep my strength up, this
work will one day be written" (212): letter of February 14, 1950 (one week after Hannah Arendt's visit to
Freiburg), the only one beginning *Meine liebe Frau* (My
dear wife).

5. HEIDEGGER'S WOMEN

1. *Epektasis,* a term originally used by Gregory of Nyssa,
describes "the soul's eternal movement into God's infinite being," as J. Warren Smith explains in "John Wesley's Growth in Grace and Gregory of Nyssa's Epectasy:
A Conversation in Dynamic Perfection," *Bulletin of the
John Rylands Library* 85, nos. 2–3 (2003): 348. —Trans.

2. While that phrase appears as "My dearest Soul" in the
English edition of the letters, I have chosen to translate

it as "My dear little soul," which takes into account, as the French translation does, the diminutive included in the German noun *Seelchen*. —Trans.

3. The phrase *femme légitime,* used here to refer to Simone de Beauvoir, is less problematic in French, which makes no distinction between "woman" and "wife," than in English. As Simone de Beauvoir was not Sartre's lawful wife, she is frequently described in English as his "life partner," with an implied sense of legitimacy. —Trans.

4. Jean-Paul Sartre, *Witness to My Life: The Letters of Jean-Paul Sartre to Simone de Beauvoir, 1926–1939,* ed. Simone de Beauvoir and trans. L. Fahnestock and N. MacAfee (New York: Scribner, 1992).

5. Hannah Arendt and Martin Heidegger. *Letters, 1925–1975,* ed. Ursula Ludz and trans. Andrew Shields (New York: Harcourt, 2003), 9.

6. *Saint* is the predicate of the woman insofar as she gives herself, the correlate of the "yes," or, at any rate, it was the predicate, during the same years, of both Elfride and the Hannah she knew nothing about: "And your great hour—when you become a saint—when you stand completely revealed [. . .] but [you are a] saint—may you preserve this shyness—may his [God's] "yes" preserve you" (ibid., 20–21).

7. Ibid., 78.

8. Martin often signed his letters to Elfride "Your little Blackamoor," a nickname she had given him in reference to his dark complexion. Here the abbreviation stands for "white Blackamoor," meaning that his hair was by then white. —Trans.

9. Since the noun *sainte* and the adjective *sainte* are written identically in French, their use in a given sentence is sometimes equivocal. English, on the other hand, requires distinguishing between *saint* and *saintly* (or *holy,* as in "the Holy Virgin," *la Sainte Vierge,* or even *sacred*). Thus what I have translated as "they are both ways of being a saint" could also have been rendered as "they are both ways of being holy/saintly" (*d'être sainte*). —Trans.

7. COUPLES FROM FRANCE AND GERMANY

1. Hannah Arendt and Martin Heidegger, *Letters, 1925–1975,* ed. Ursula Ludz and trans. Andrew Shields (New York: Harcourt, 2003), 6.
2. Ibid., 6.
3. Ibid., 87.
4. Jean-Paul Sartre, *Witness to My Life: The Letters of Jean-Paul Sartre to Simone de Beauvoir, 1926–1939,* ed.

Simone de Beauvoir and trans. L. Fahnestock and N. MacAfee (New York: Scribner, 1992), 199. Tania was the pseudonym of Wanda Kosawiewicz. —Trans.

5. Ibid., 203. Particularly in classical French theater, *flamme* referred to a passionate love (cf. *déclarer sa flamme,* to declare one's love). — Trans.

8. LINGUISTIC TRANSFIGURATION

1. *Beying,* an antiquated spelling of *being,* has been used in some English translations of Heidegger to render *Seyn,* the old spelling of *Sein* in German. —Trans.

2. By placing in the mouth of his teenage protagonist Sortebeker such lines as "The rat withdraws itself by unconcealing itself into the ratty. So the rat errates the ratty, illuminating it with errancy. For the ratty has come-to-be in the errancy where the rat errs and so fosters error," Gunter Grass wickedly parodied Heideggerese in his novel *Dog Years*, originally published in 1963, English translation by Ralph Mannheim (Harcourt, Brace and World, 1965). In *The Jargon of Authenticity,* originally published in 1964, English translation by Knut Tarnowski and Frederic Will (Northwestern University Press, 1973), T. W. Adorno critiqued the

language of Heidegger and other existentialists as "giv[ing] itself over to the market, to balderdash, or to the predominating vulgarity." —Trans.

3. The phrase "seized by rectoral debauchery" is an allusion to the title of Jules Romains's 1923 play *Monsieur Le Trouhadec saisi par la débauche* (Monsieur Le Trouhadec seized by debauchery). —Trans.

4. The console table figures in the last strophe of the sonnet "Tout Orgueil fume-t-il du soir," in Stéphane Mallarmé, *Oeuvres complètes,* ed. Henri Mondor and G. Jean-Aubry (Paris: Gallimard-Pléiade, 1945), 73. —Trans.

Bibliography

Arendt, Hannah. *The Portable Hannah Arendt*. Ed. Peter
    Baehr. London: Penguin, 2003.

——, and Martin Heidegger. *Letters, 1925–1975*. Ed. Ursula
    Ludz and trans. Andrew Shields. New York: Harcourt,
    2003.

Amato, Massimo, Philippe Arjakovsky, Marcel Conche,
    et al. *Heidegger, à plus forte raison*. Ed. François Fédier.
    Paris: Fayard, 2007.

Faye, Emmanuel. *Heidegger: The Introduction of Nazism Into
    Philosophy*. Trans. Michael B. Smith. New Haven: Yale
    University Press, 2009.

Fédier, François. *Heidegger: Anatomie d'un scandale*. Paris:
    Robert Laffont, 1988.

——, ed. *Heidegger, à plus forte raison*. Paris: Fayard, 2007.

Gilson, Étienne. *Choir of Muses*. Trans. Maisie Ward. Lon-
    don: Sheed and Ward, 1953.

Heidegger, Martin. *Letters to His Wife.* Ed. Gertrud Heidegger and trans. R. D. V. Glasgow. Cambridge: Polity,
2008.

——. *"Ma chère petite âme". Lettres à sa femme Elfride,
1915–1970.* Trans. Marie-Ange Maillet. Paris: Seuil, 2007.

——. *The Question Concerning Technology and Other Essays.*
Trans. William Lovitt. New York: Harper and Row, 1982.

Husserl, Edmund. *Die Krisis der europaischen Wissenschaften
und die transzendentale Phänomenologie.* Ed. Walter
Biemel. The Hague: Martinus Nijhoff, 1976.

Joris, Pierre. "Heidegger, France, Politics, the University."
http://wings.buffalo.edu/epc/authors/joris/heideggerfas-
cism.html.

Klemperer, Victor. *The Language of the Third Reich.* Trans.
Martin Brady. London: Continuum, 2006.

Mallarmé, Stéphane. *Oeuvres complètes.* Ed. Henri Mondor
and G. Jean-Aubry. Paris: Gallimard-Pléiade, 1945.

Plato. *Cratylus. Parmenides. Greater Hippias. Lesser Hippias.*
Trans. H. N. Fowler. Loeb Classical Library. Cambridge:
Harvard University Press, 1926.

Sartre, Jean-Paul. *Witness to My Life: The Letters of Jean-Paul
Sartre to Simone de Beauvoir, 1926–1939.* Ed. Simone de
Beauvoir and trans. L. Fahnestock and N. MacAfee.
New York: Scribner, 1992.

Smith, J. Warren. "John Wesley's Growth in Grace and
     Gregory of Nyssa's Epectasy: A Conversation in
     Dynamic Perfection." *Bulletin of the John Rylands Library*
     85, nos. 2–3 (2003): 347–57.

Index

Absolute, 2; *see also* Truth

Adorno, T. W., 60–61, 74*n*2

Affairs, 14–15; with Arendt, 30, 44, 53–54; of E. Heidegger, 42–43, 55; with Putscher, 38, 40; of Sartre, 53–58; *see also* Women

Âme, 57–58

Anti-Semitism, vii–viii; in letters, to wife, 17–18, 23–27

Aquinas, Thomas, 2

Arendt, Hannah, 65*n*1; affair with, 30, 44, 53–54; on great thinkers, 2–3; on M. Heidegger, 2–3, 10; on Jewishness, ix; letters to, 25–26, 41–42, 44, 53–54; in local disagreement 2, 9–11; on Plato, 2–3, 10

Aristotle: as great thinker, 4; *Metaphysics*, ix–x; on ontology, ix–x; politics relating to, 6

Art, xii

Badiou, Alain, vii–viii; on being, xii; *Being and Event*, xii–xiii, xiv–xv; Cassin compared to, viii, xvi–xix; M. Heidegger

Badiou, Alain (*continued*) relating to, ix, xi–xv, 63*n*4, 64*n*8; on knowledge, xiv; on language and Nazism, 22–23; on local disagreement 1, 5–7; on local disagreement 2, 10–13; on local disagreement 3, 13–14; on local disagreement 4, 22–23; *Manifesto for Philosophy*, 64*n*8; on mathematics, xii, xiii–xv; on Nazism, 6, 7, 22–23; "On the Creative Correlation Between the Great and the Little," xviii–xix, 14–15; on ontology, xi–xii, 13; on poetry, xiv–xv; on political philosophy, 5–6, 10–11; on politics, xvi–xvii; on sexual difference, xvii–xix; on truth, xii–xiv; on women, 46–47

Bauer, Walter, 24

Beauvoir, Simone de, 41, 53–58

Being, xi; Badiou on, xii; *Dasein* relating to, xiv; M. Heidegger on, xiv

Being and Event (Badiou), xii–xiii; Meditation II, xiv–xv

Bergson, Henri, 27

Blanchot, Maurice, 22–23

Bosteels, Bruno, 64*n*6

Brown, Gordon, 27

Caesar, Friedel, 42–43

Career, 49–51

Cassin, Barbara, vii–viii; Badiou compared to, viii, xvi–xix; Char and, ix, xi, 19–20; on great thinkers, 3–4; M. Heidegger, relating to, ix, xi; on E. Heidegger, 45–46; Jewishness and, ix; on local disagreement 1, 3–4; on local disagreement 2, 10–13; on local disagreement 3, 13–14; on local disagreement 4, 19–20; on logology, ix, x–xi, xviii, 13; on Nazism, 6–7; "On the Creative Correlation Between the Great and the Little," xviii–xix, 14–15; on ontology, ix–x; on political philosophy, 3–4; on politics, xvi–xvii; on sexual difference, xvii–xix; on women, 13, 45–46

Cassirer, Ernst, 21

Celan, Paul, 20, 69*n*4

Censorship, 15

Char, René, 64*n*8; Cassin and, ix, xi, 19–20; M. Heidegger and, 20, 68*n*2

Chirac, Jacques, 27

Communication, x–xi

Comte, Auguste, 1–2

Contemplative life, 3–4

Couple, 55–56

Dasein, xiv

Deconstruction, 12

Deleuze, Gilles, 8

Denazification process, 18

Derrida, Jacques, 8

Descartes, René, 1–2

Diderot, Denis, 10–11

Epektasis, 73*n*1
Existentialism, 55–56

Faye, Emmanuel, 9, 66*n*4
Fédier, François, ix, 9, 66*n*4
Feick, Hildegard, 44–45
Femininity, 13–14
Fichte, Johann Gottlieb, 1–2
Flamme (flame), 57–58, 74*n*5
Foucault, Michel, 8
French Heideggerians, 22–23
French language, 21–22
French philosophical production, 7–8

German language, 21–23; *see also* Language
German University, 50, 70*n*9
Geschichtlich, 65*n*2
Gilson, Étienne, 36
Grass, Günter, 60, 74*n*2
Great, The, xviii–xx, 30, 41
Great thinkers, xvi; Arendt on, 2–3; Aristotle as, 4; Cassin on, 3–4; in human affairs, 3–5, 10; in local disagreement 1, 3–9; political philosophy relating to, 1–9
Gregory of Nyssa, 71*n*1

Hegel, Georg Wilhelm Friedrich, 6, 22; *ThePhilosophy of History*, 66*n*5

Heidegger, Elfride, vii; affairs of, 42–43, 55; Cassin on, 45–46; courtship of, 35–37; on Jews, 17; marriage to, 39–43; on Putscher affair, 40; religious affiliations and, 37–38; *see also* Letters, to wife

Heidegger, Fritz, 40

Heidegger, Gertrud, 14, 17–18

Heidegger, Hermann, 42–43, 55

Heidegger, Martin: Arendt on, 2–3, 10; Badiou relating to, ix, xi–xv, 63*n*4, 64*n*8; on being, xiv; Cassin relating to, ix, xi; Char and, 20, 68*n*2; controversy surrounding, in France, 7–9, 32–33; critics of, viii; on *Dasein*, xiv; on mathematics, xiii; on politics and philosophy, xvi–xvii; politics of, viii, xvi–xvii, 49–51; postwar activities of, 18–19; Sartre compared to, 53–58; on truth, xii–xiii; women and, 14–15, 30, 35–36, 38–47, 54–58; *see also specific topics*; *specific works*

Heraclitus, 60

Hero, 66*n*5

Historial, 65*n*2

Historie, 65*n*2

Hölderlin, Friedrich, 66*n*3

Home, 39–40

Human affairs, 3–5, 10

Humboldt, Alexander von, 60
Husserl, Edmund, 22, 24
Hysteric, xvii–xviii, 13–14

Jaspers, Karl, 25
Jewishness, ix
Jews, 17; *see also* Anti-Semitism; Nazism
Jollivet, Simone, 41
Joris, Pierre, 69*n*9
Jüdische Rundschau, 25

Kant, Immanuel, 3, 6
Klemperer, Victor, 21, 69*n*6
Knowledge, xi, xiv

Lacoue-Labarthe, Philippe, 27
Language, x–xi; French, 21–22; German, 21–22; Nazism relating to, 21–23; Plato on, 22; translations of, 21–22, 59–62, 65*n*2
Lautman, Albert, 8
Leibniz, Gottfried Wilhelm von, 1–2
Letters: to Arendt, 25–26, 41–42, 44, 53–54; to wife, vii–viii; anti-Semitism in, 17–18, 23–27; approach to reading, 17–18; on career, 49–51; disappearance of, 18, 23–24; last letter, 39; *Ma chère petite âme: Lettres de Martin Heidegger à sa*

femme Elfride 1915–1970, vii; *Mein liebes Seelchen! Briefe Martin Heideggers an seine Frau Elfride 1915–1970*, vii; National Socialism in, 18; Nazism in, 17, 29–33; "On the Creative Correlation Between the Great and the Little," xviii–xix, 14–15; philosophical import of, 61–62; selection of, 17–18; sexual difference in relation to, xviii–xix

Letters to His Wife: 1915–1970 (M. Heidegger), vii

Little, The, xviii–xx, 30, 41–42, 57–58, 67*n*7

Local disagreement 1: Badiou on, 5–7; Cassin on, 3–4; great thinkers in, 3–9; on Nazism, 6–9

Local disagreement 2: Arendt in, 9–11; Badiou on, 10–13; Cassin on, 10–13; on Nazism, 9–11; on One, 9–13

Local disagreement 3: Badiou on, 13–14; Cassin on, 13–14; women in, 13–15

Local disagreement 4: Badiou on, 22–23; Cassin on, 19–20; on Nazism, 19–23; on translations, 21–22

Localization, xiv

Logology, ix, x–xi, xviii, 13

Logos, 7

L'Ordre philosophique, 14

Love, xii

Ma chère petite âme: Lettres de Martin Heidegger à sa femme Elfride 1915–1970 (M. Heidegger), vii

Malebranche, Nicolas, 1–2

Mallarmé, Stéphane, 62, 77*n*4

Manifesto for Philosophy (Badiou), 64*n*8

Marriage, 39–43; *see also* Heidegger, Elfride; Letters, to wife

Masculinity, 13–14

Master, xvii–xviii, 13–14

Mathematics: Badiou on, xii, xiii–xv; M. Heidegger on, xiii; ontology and, xii, xv

Mein liebes Seelchen! Briefe Martin Heideggers an seine Frau Elfride 1915–1970 (M. Heidegger), vii

Merleau-Ponty, Maurice, 8

Metaphysics, 12–13

Metaphysics (Aristotle), ix–x

Morality, 27

Nancy, Jean-Luc, 22–23

National Socialism, viii, 1; in letters, to wife, 18

Nazism, vii–viii, 1, 14; apology and repentance for, 19–20, 27–28; Badiou on, 6, 7, 22–23; Cassin on, 6–7; controversy around, 7–9; denazification process, 18; language relating to, 21–23; in letters, to wife, 17, 29–33; local disagreement 1 on, 6–9; local disagreement 2 on, 9–11; local disagreement 4 on, 19–23; silence on, 25–27; *see also* Anti-Semitism

Nietzsche, Friedrich Wilhelm, 22, 31, 61

Noncontradiction, x

Obama, Barack, 27

One, The, 9–13

"On the Creative Correlation Between the Great and the Little" (Badiou and Cassin), xviii–xix, 14–15

Ontology: Aristotle on, ix–x; Badiou on, xi–xii, 13; Cassin on, ix–x; mathematics and, xii, xv

Parmenides, 12, 60

"Patmos" (Hölderlin), 66n3

Philosophy: four conditions of, xii; French philosophical production, 7–8; poetry and, xiv–xv, 64n8; politics and, vii–viii, xii, xvi–xvii, 1–3, 5; see also Political philosophy

Philosophy of History, The (Hegel), 66n5

Phronimos, 4

Planetary prose, 35–38

Plato, 9; Arendt on, 2–3, 10; on language, 22; on poetry, xiv; on truth, xiii

Podewils, Sophie Dorothée von, 43–44

Poetry: Badiou on, xiv–xv; philosophy and, xiv–xv, 64n8; Plato on, xiv

Polis, 7

Political philosophy: Badiou on, 5–6, 10–11; Cassin on, 3–4; great thinkers relating to, 1–9

Politics: Aristotle relating to, 6; Badiou on, xvi–xvii; career and, 49–51; Cassin on, xvi–xvii; of M. Heidegger, viii,

Politics (*continued*) xvi–xvii, 49–51; Kant relating to, 6; philosophy and, vii–viii, xii, xvi–xvii, 1–3, 5; truth relating to, xvi–xvii, 2–3, 5, 6–7
Popper, Karl, 9
Postwar activities, 18–19
Principle of noncontradiction, x
Putscher, Marielene, 38, 40

Religion, 27
Religious affiliations, 37–38
Revolutionaries, 27
Roaring Twenties, 55–56
Rousseau, Jean-Jacques, 1–2

Sachsen-Meiningen, Margot von, 43–44
Saint, 44–47, 72n6, 73n9
Sartre, Jean-Paul, 41; M. Heidegger compared to, 53–58
Schopenhauer, Arthur, 1–2
Science, xii
Sexual difference: Badiou on, xvii–xix; Cassin on, xvii–xix; letters to wife in relation to, xviii–xix; women and, xvii–xix
She Came to Stay (de Beauvoir), 55
Sophists, ix, xi, 12–13
Sophos, 4

Thales, 4

Translations, 21–22, 59–62, 65*n*2

Truong, Nicolas, ix

Trust, 42–43

Truth, xi; Badiou on, xii–xiv; M. Heidegger on, xii–xiii; Plato on, xiii; politics relating to, xvi–xvii, 2–3, 5, 6–7

Tyrants, 2–3

University, German, 50, 69–70*n*9

Valet, 10, 68*n*5

Védrine, Louise, 41, 57–58

Vidal-Naquet, Pierre, 19–20, 69*n*3

Vietta, Dory, 44–45

Whole, The, 11–13

Women, vii–viii, 12; Badiou on, 46–47; Cassin on, 13, 45–46; M. Heidegger and, 14–15, 30, 35–36, 38–47, 54–58; hypothesis 1 on, 45–46; hypothesis 2 on, 46–47; in local disagreement 3, 13–15; as saint, 44–47, 72*n*5, 73*n*8; sexual difference and, xvii–xix; typology of, 43–44

INSURRECTIONS:

CRITICAL STUDIES IN RELIGION, POLITICS, AND CULTURE
Slavoj Žižek, Clayton Crockett, Creston Davis, Jeffrey W.
Robbins, Editors

After the Death of God, John D. Caputo and Gianni
    Vattimo, edited by Jeffrey W. Robbins
The Politics of Postsecular Religion: Mourning Secular Futures,
    Ananda Abeysekara
Nietzsche and Levinas: "After the Death of a Certain God,"
    edited by Jill Stauffer and Bettina Bergo
*Strange Wonder: The Closure of Metaphysics and the Opening
    of Awe,* Mary-Jane Rubenstein
*Religion and the Specter of the West: Sikhism, India,
    Postcoloniality, and the Politics of Translation,*
    Arvind Mandair
*Plasticity at the Dusk of Writing: Dialectic, Destruction,
    Deconstruction,* Catherine Malabou

Anatheism: Returning to God After God, Richard Kearney

Rage and Time: A Psychopolitical Investigation, Peter
    Sloterdijk

*Radical Political Theology: Religion and Politics After
    Liberalism,* Clayton Crockett

Radical Democracy and Political Theology, Jeffrey W. Robbins

Hegel and the Infinite: Religion, Politics, and Dialectic, edited
    by Slavoj Žižek, Clayton Crockett, and Creston Davis

What Does a Jew Want? On Binationalism and Other Specters,
    Udi Aloni

A Radical Philosophy of Saint Paul, Stanislas Breton, edited
    by Ward Blanton, translated by Joseph N. Ballan

Hermeneutic Communism: From Heidegger to Marx, Gianni
    Vattimo and Santiago Zabala

Deleuze Beyond Badiou: Ontology, Multiplicity, and Event,
    Clayton Crockett

*Self and Emotional Life: Philosophy, Psychoanalysis, and
    Neuroscience,* Adrian Johnston and Catherine Malabou

*The Incident at Antioch: A Tragedy in Three Acts / L'Incident
    d'Antioche: Tragédie en trois actes,* Alain Badiou,
    translated by Susan Spitzer

Philosophical Temperaments: From Plato to Foucault, Peter
    Sloterdijk

To Carl Schmitt: Letters and Reflections, Jacob Taubes,
    translated by Keith Tribe

Encountering Religion: Responsibility and Criticism After Secularism, Tyler Roberts

Spinoza for Our Time: Politics and Postmodernity, Antonio Negri, translated by William McCuaig

Factory of Strategy: Thirty-three Lessons on Lenin, Antonio Negri, translated by Arianna Bove

Cut of the Real: Subjectivity in Poststructuralism Philosophy, Katerina Kolozova

A Materialism for the Masses: Saint Paul and the Philosophy of Undying Life, Ward Blanton

Our Broad Present: Time and Contemporary Culture, Hans Ulrich Gumbrecht

Wrestling with the Angel: Experiments in Symbolic Life, Tracy McNulty

Cloud of the Impossible: Negative Theology and Planetary Entanglements, Catherine Keller

What Does Europe Want? The Union and Its Discontents, Slavoj Žižek and Srećko Horvat

Nietzsche Versus Paul, Abed Azzam

Paul's Summons to Messianic Life: Political Theology and the Coming Awakening, L. L. Welborn

Reimagining the Sacred: Richard Kearney Debates God with James Wood, Catherine Keller, Charles Taylor, Julia Kristeva, Gianni Vattimo, Simon Critchley, Jean-Luc Marion, John Caputo, David Tracy, Jens Zimmermann,

and Merold Westphal, edited by Richard Kearney and
Jens Zimmermann

*An Insurrectionist Manifesto: Four New Gospels for a Radical
Politics,* Ward Blanton, Clayton Crockett, Jeffrey W.
Robbins, and Noëlle Vahanian

Milton Keynes UK
Ingram Content Group UK Ltd.
UKHW030733151024
449648UK00004B/115